1906

1906

SURVIVING SAN FRANCISCO'S

GREAT EARTHQUAKE

AND FIRE

By
GERSTLE MACK

with an Introduction by

Dianne Feinstein
Mayor of San Francisco

CHRONICLE BOOKS

Library of Congress Cataloging in Publication Data

Mack, Gerstle, 1894 .
   1906: surviving the great earthquake and fire.

   Bibliography: p.
   Includes index.
   1. San Francisco (Calif.)—Earthquake and fire, 1906—
Personal narratives. 2. Mack, Gerstle, 1894–
F869.S357M25   979.4'61051   81-1660
ISBN 0-87701-176-1 (pbk.)

Photo Credits:
   California Historical Society, pages 25, 27, 28, 29, 30, 33,
      34, 39, 41, 42, 44–45, 47, 48, 50, 53, 57, 64, 66, 67, 69,
      70, 108, 118, 119
   San Francisco *Chronicle* Archives, pages 92, 101, 111

Editing and design by Harper & Vandenburgh.
Composition by HMS Typographers.
Printing by Peter G. Levison and Associates.

Chronicle Books
870 Market Street
San Francisco, CA 94102

INTRODUCTION

In April of this year San Francisco commemorates the 75th anniversary of the Great Earthquake and Fire of 1906, a natural disaster which claimed some 500 lives and which left our city in rubble and ashes.

But, like the phoenix of ancient mythology, San Francisco arose from its ashes and renewed itself as one of the world's most beautiful and remarkable cities. San Francisco is renowned as Everybody's Favorite City, and people who have been here, even for only a brief visit, discover that some small part of their hearts is always left in San Francisco.

Gerstle Mack's newest book, *1906: SURVIVING SAN FRANCISCO'S GREAT EARTHQUAKE AND FIRE*, provides a rare and personal glimpse into those substrata qualities of character which typified our population at the turn of the twentieth century, and which accounted for what historians everywhere regard as one of the urban renewal miracles of modern times. These were people who were literally building the West with the strength of their own hands and with an imaginative vision of our nation's future. Their blood lines throbbed with vitality, ingenuity, resiliency, and a full measure of the kind of stamina required to get beyond calamity to work together for a better tomorrow.

As a born and bred San Franciscan, Gerstle Mack is superbly qualified to reach back into his early adolescence in order to describe vividly to contemporary readers how the city reeled beneath the worst disaster in its history. His eyewitness account of the impact of the earthquake and fire upon his family and their friends and neighbors gives his book a breadth of personal experience that is often minimized or omitted in the still-growing library of works on this momentous event. He is particularly adept in portraying both the compassion for others and the toughness and determination evinced by San Franciscans of 1906 in their willingness and eagerness to pull together as a team in order to rebuild their beloved city.

These are qualities still vital to us today. As such, Gerstle's recollections are not merely matters of record but also threads which help to hold together the very fabric of our heritage. Through Gerstle's easy-to-read and natural narrative prose with its rich lode of anecdotes, we enter a time in our past which enables us to better understand those rather intangible yet elemental powers upon which our survival as a civilization ultimately depends. We see how people can respond sensitively and intelligently to an unsuspected blow from nature, and we are reminded that the men and women whose abilities, common sense, and courage create the magic that *is* San Francisco remain our greatest resource.

DIANNE FEINSTEIN
Mayor of San Francisco

ACKNOWLEDGMENTS

I am deeply indebted to my nephew, James Mack Gerstley, for invaluable assistance in connection with the publication of this book. To my brother, Harold Lewis Mack, for personal recollections. To Mr. and Mrs. Thomas Carr Howe for the loan of a book by James W. Byrne, Recollections of the Fire, *which helped to explain the escape of most of the Kohl Building from destruction by fire. To Maraldine McCubbin, Assistant Vice President of the Crocker National Bank, for information concerning the old Crocker Building. To James E. Moss, Executive Director of the California Historical Society, San Francisco, for reading the manuscript. To Mrs. Martha H. Kennedy, Curator of Photographs of the California Historical Society, and to Mrs. Joy Berry, Mrs. Jocelyn Moss, Mrs. M. K. Swingle, and Laura O'Keefe, librarians of that Society, for their courteous, efficient, and time-saving help in locating photographs in the Society's collection to serve as illustrations. To John W. Mifflin for useful introductions and for his unfailing interest in the progress of this work. To John Foster White, Jr., for his generous help in my search for relevant material in the Bay Area.*

G. M.

1906

~~

SOME PERSONAL RECOLLECTIONS

In April 1906 I was not quite twelve years old. My parents, Adolph and Clara Gerstle Mack, had commissioned the architectural firm of Newsom and Newsom to design and supervise the construction of a new house at 2676 Pacific Avenue, between Pierce and Scott streets. Building was begun in the autumn of 1904, and we moved into the completed residence in October 1905, just six months before the earthquake. I was very much the youngest of four children and the only one then living with my parents. My older sister, with her husband and seven-weeks-old infant son, had her own house at 2209 Buchanan Street, between Sacramento and Clay. My brother was a stockbroker in New York, and my younger sister had married an English cousin and lived in London.

Throughout my childhood I had felt many minor and some moderately severe earthquakes and had come to accept them as routine features of San Francisco life. Therefore, when I was suddenly awakened at 5:13 on the morning of April 18, I was not frightened, although I realized after the first few seconds that this quake was far more powerful than any I had previously experienced. My bed, which was placed with its headboard against one wall, was shifted into the middle of the room and turned counterclockwise about ninety degrees. Many people afterwards claimed that the quake was accompanied by rumbling noises deep in the earth. I heard nothing of that kind, but there was plenty of noise in my room

1906

~~

from another source. On the mantel above the fireplace I had accumulated an assortment of tiny animals and other knick-knacks of various materials, then known as an "inch collection." Most of these fell onto the tiled hearth, where some bounced and others broke. The only noise I heard was the clatter of this cascade of falling miniatures.

I stayed in bed until the floor stopped heaving. A few minutes later my father came into my room, and I remember saying something like: "Gee! That was a good one!" Father told me to get dressed and to go downstairs, where I joined my parents. The shock had greatly upset my mother, but she concealed her nervousness and took charge of the household with her usual efficiency. The cook and the two maids lived on the top floor; the Chinese laundryman had his room and bath in the basement. Mother gathered them all together on the ground floor, where her calm manner allayed any incipient hysteria.

For some odd reason I have no recollection whatever of eating or drinking anything that whole first day, though we must have had meals of some kind; probably cold, picnic fashion, as we realized almost at once that the earthquake had probably damaged the kitchen chimney so that it was unsafe to light a fire. That danger was confirmed as soon as we ventured out of doors. One of the most conspicuous features of our house was another chimney, eight feet wide, which extended from basement to roof on the Pacific Avenue front, with fireplaces opening on three of the four floors. This great chimney had separated from the house and had fallen across the street in scattered heaps of brick and plaster. Fortunately it had fallen away from the house; if it had toppled inward we should all have been killed or at least seriously injured. That was the only structural damage. Indoors there was some breakage of crockery and glassware shaken off the pantry shelves. In the library dozens of books had spilled from the open shelves onto the carpet, arranging themselves in neat

1906

~~

curved rows like decks of cards spread out for inspection before dealing, indicating that the earthquake's complex movements included a distinct rotary twist.

We very soon discovered that electric lights, gas jets, and telephones were out of commission. We filled one or two bathtubs with water that had accumulated in the house pipes, but the flow quickly diminished to a trickle and then stopped altogether; the earthquake had broken almost all of the city water mains. My father and I walked to my sister's house and were relieved to find that she, her husband, and her infant son were unhurt and her house had suffered no damage except possibly cracked chimneys. I walked home to reassure my mother that my sister and her family were all safe, while my father continued on his way downtown (on foot, as all street-cars had stopped running) to see what had happened to his business premises.

At that time he was president of a wholesale drug firm, Mack & Company, which occupied a six-story brick building at 13-15 Fremont Street, half a block south of Market Street and five short blocks from the Ferry Building. By the time he reached Fremont Street that morning the fire, started simultaneously in various places by the earthquake, had been burning for several hours, and the whole district was ablaze. The flames and scorching heat prevented a close inspection, but my father could see that the building had already been completely gutted, though most of the outer walls still remained upright.

My own recollections of that Wednesday are somewhat sketchy, and I cannot account for every hour in orderly sequence. I do clearly remember two events. During the afternoon my mother, my father, and I spent some time in Lafayette Square, a small oasis crowning one of the hilltops about ten blocks from our house, whence the clouds of smoke from the burning city were clearly visible and we could watch the progress of the conflagration. Most of the flaming buildings

1906

~~

downtown were hidden from us by the bulk of Nob Hill, but some could be seen blazing fiercely south of Market Street. My other most vivid memory is of a similar vigil after dark from Alta Plaza, another high park in the hilly city, only one block from our house. By that time the fire had spread north, south, and west, and flames as well as towering clouds of smoke could be seen against the red glow of the eastern sky.

There had been several minor aftershocks during the day, and my mother suggested that we should sleep on the ground floor that night so that we could leave the house quickly and not be trapped upstairs if another big quake should occur. We dragged mattresses and bedding downstairs and slept, half dressed, on the floor of the living room. At least I, a healthy twelve-year-old, slept soundly. I suspect that my parents spent a less restful night.

The earthquake took place during the Easter vacation of the public schools. I was then in my final year at Pacific Heights Grammar School and in normal circumstances would have graduated at the end of May, ready to enter Lowell High School in the early autumn. But all schools remained closed for the rest of the spring term, and we received our diplomas many months later at a ceremony held in Golden Gate Park.

My maternal grandmother, Hannah Gerstle, who was then in Europe with my two older aunts, owned an eleven-acre country place in San Rafael in Marin County, about fifteen miles north of San Francisco, across the bay. Usually it was occupied by various members of the family from the middle of May until the end of September. On the day of the quake my parents, in agreement with my two younger aunts and their husbands, who lived in adjoining houses two blocks from our own house, decided that all of the women and children of the family should go to San Rafael the next day. It was a wise decision. Nobody could predict how far the fire would spread or whether any of our houses would survive. (In

1906

~~

fact, though, all family residences, located some distance west of the limits of the burned area, were saved except three handsome houses on the east side of Van Ness Avenue between Pine and California streets, belonging to my grandmother's sister, Sarah Sloss, her daughter, and one of her sons. These houses were "backfired"—that is, they were deliberately burned down in a desperate, and ultimately successful, effort to prevent the fire from advancing more than one block west of wide Van Ness Avenue.)

Another reason for the exodus of the women and children was the threat of famine in the city (which fortunately did not materialize); but at best the lack of electricity, gas, running water, and indoor cooking facilities would have made life exceedingly uncomfortable for many weeks, if not months.

Transportation to the Ferry Building was a problem. No streetcars were running, nobody in our immediate family owned a carriage and horses, and practically every vehicle, from elegant victorias to smelly garbage wagons, had already been hired. In 1906 automobiles were still scarce in San Francisco, but luckily my youngest aunt had a brother-in-law, Herbert Fleishhacker, who owned two chauffeur-driven touring cars, one of which he generously placed at the disposal of our family. Into this car, on Thursday morning, squeezed my aunt and her seven-months-old daughter, my sister and her infant son, my mother and myself, and (I think) nurses for the two babies, plus one small suitcase apiece. The only route to the Ferry Building not blocked by the fire ran east on Pacific Avenue to Van Ness Avenue, north on Van Ness (which, having buckled and cracked wide open in several places, presented a challenge to the driver's skill) to Bay Street, then east and southeast past the docks that fringed the waterfront. At the Ferry Building we found the ferryboats, crowded with refugees from the blazing city, running on more or less normal schedules to Oakland and Alameda on the east side of the

1906

～～

bay and to Sausalito and Tiburon in Marin County. Local commuter trains were also operating at regular intervals, so we all arrived in San Rafael with little trouble or delay. My other aunt then living in San Francisco crossed the bay that same morning in a tugboat chartered by her husband, and joined us in San Rafael with her three young sons, aged from nine years to fifteen months, her husband's father and sister, and two or three servants.

San Rafael had been well shaken by the earthquake but had suffered little damage except cracked chimneys, always the most vulnerable elements in the earthquake zone. On the Gerstle property there were three houses in addition to a servants' "cottage" containing a laundry, and a combined stable and cowbarn. During the winter preceding the quake the newest and largest of the three family residences had been moved from its hilltop site to a more accessible and convenient location near the bottom of the garden. When the earthquake struck, this house had already been set on its new foundations, but there was still a good deal of work to be done, and the house would not be habitable for three or four weeks after our arrival. Meanwhile the women and children of the family, plus various in-laws in need of shelter, were crowded into the two smaller houses.

We were uncomfortable but safe, and there were many amenities here that were lacking in San Francisco. San Rafael was untouched by fire; electricity, gas, telephones, and running water were available; the shops were well stocked with food; and we had our own horses and carriages, including a large station wagon or "carryall," in charge of our efficient coachman Fred Wright. Within the next day or two a few more servants drifted over from the city, but lack of space reduced their number considerably below the normal quota. The family members made their own beds and dusted their own rooms. One of the two habitable houses contained only bedrooms and one or two baths, so the entire colony, general-

13

1906

~~

ly numbering between twenty-five and thirty people excluding servants and babies, all ate together in one large dining room in the "main" house. The most serious problem involved cooking; with the kitchen chimney unusable until it had been inspected and, if necessary, repaired, all cooking was done on a makeshift stove carried into the cement-paved back yard. The stove was not large, and if it had an oven at all it must have been a very small one, so that almost everything had to be cooked on top of the stove. That eliminated all roasting, baking, and broiling, and restricted our menus to an assortment of meat-and-vegetable stews or vast amounts of chopped beef in the form of hamburgers. My mother, as the senior member of the group, ran the commissary and drove every morning to the "village" to buy food for the entire establishment. There was little ready cash and all banks were closed for a month after the quake, but we had had charge accounts for years in all the shops so we had no financial problems.

Almost every evening one or more husbands came over from the city to dine and spend the night and to enjoy the luxury of hot baths, unavailable in San Francisco. These unheralded visits usually involved some reshuffling of sleeping arrangements, but somehow or other beds were found for everyone. My father came as often as he could, two or three times a week. He was working hard in the city trying to wind up the complicated affairs of Mack & Company (which never resumed operations) and to begin the long and difficult negotiations with insurance companies that occupied the time and attention of most San Francisco businessmen for the next two or three years. The fire had burned right through the iron safe in the drug firm's office, and every scrap of paper, the records of many years, had been destroyed. The company had sold drugs and related merchandise—about fourteen thousand different items—to hundreds of retail stores throughout California and all of the states west of the Rockies; but not a single

∿

memorandum of these transactions had survived the fire.

A few days after the quake my father, one of his brothers, and another partner, in addition to the bookkeeper, Fred Kellogg, gathered round a table and listed the names and addresses of as many of the firm's retail buyers as they could remember, and then sent a printed form letter to each, explaining that all sales records had been destroyed and requesting every retailer to inform Mack & Company how much his store owed and to remit payment as soon as convenient. The replies testified to the honesty and integrity of the firm's customers. The partners estimated that ninety-five percent of the drugstores promptly sent statements of their debts, usually accompanied by checks; and in some instances retailers paid what they owed even before they received the requests from Mack & Company. Of the approximately five percent that did not pay, most were local San Francisco dealers whose records had also been destroyed and who, in any event, had little or nothing left with which to pay their debts.

My twenty-one-year-old brother Harold had been in San Francisco for several days on business for his firm of stockbrokers, and had started back to New York on Monday, April 16, two days before the earthquake. News of the disaster, very inaccurate and greatly exaggerated, reached him when the Overland Limited stopped at Omaha on Wednesday evening. He continued his journey as far as Chicago, where he arrived on Thursday morning. There he went to his firm's branch office, borrowed several thousand dollars, and sent a cable to our sister in London saying in effect: "Family all safe and gone to San Rafael." In fact he knew absolutely nothing about what had happened to his San Francisco family; we might all have been killed or gravely injured, and the entire cable, including the bit about San Rafael, was pure invention on his part. But it was inspired invention. Our English sister promptly wired the good news to our grandmother and older aunts, then traveling on the Continent; so

1906

~~~

our relatives in Europe received this reassuring information only a day or at most two days after the earthquake, and thus were spared all worry about their San Francisco families, whereas most San Franciscans living or traveling abroad had to wait many anxious days and even weeks for news of their kindred.

Harold then bought a large bottle of Horlick's malted milk tablets for his infant nephew (a bachelor uncle's idea of what a seven-weeks-old baby could digest) and, having spent only six or seven hours in Chicago, boarded the Overland Limited that same evening and returned to San Francisco. He arrived late on Sunday afternoon, April 22, and managed to get some kind of conveyance to our Pacific Avenue house, where he found our father and learned for the first time that all of the guesses that he had cabled to Europe from Chicago were actually true. He gave father the money he had brought, to be distributed among relatives and friends as needed, and then returned to the Ferry Building and arrived in San Rafael that night. There everyone had gone to bed early, but our sister heard him shouting in the garden and came downstairs in her dressing gown to let him in. All beds were occupied, so Harold spent the rest of the night on a sofa.

Early in May, three weeks after the earthquake, my mother and I went to Europe. The trip had no connection with the quake or fire. It had been planned months in advance because my sister in London was expecting her first child in July, and my mother intended to be with her during the last weeks of her pregnancy. Railroad and steamship tickets had already been bought some time before the earthquake, hotel rooms in New York had been reserved for the week or two we expected to stay there, and there seemed to be no good reason to cancel any of these arrangements.

About a week before our departure my father came to San Rafael and brought my mother and me to San Francisco

1906

〰

for one day, the only visit my mother and I had paid to the devastated city since the day after the quake. By this time the fire had long since been extinguished, much of the rubble had been cleared off the principal streets, and the long process of reconstruction had already begun. In some conveyance, either hired or provided by friends, my mother was driven from the Ferry Building to our house, where she packed trunks and suitcases with whatever we would need for the summer abroad. My father and I walked all the way home past block after block of fire-blackened ruins. We went first to look at the burned-out shell of the Mack & Company building on Fremont Street; then to the Crocker Building on Market Street, completely gutted by the fire but with its sturdy brick-and-steel frame walls intact; then uptown to Van Ness Avenue, where some of the big downtown department stores had already rented or purchased the larger undamaged residences on the west side of the avenue and had opened for business, offering for sale stock that had been en route by rail from eastern cities at the time of the quake, plus additional merchandise generously contributed by communities all over the country. I needed a new suit for traveling, having outgrown the one I was wearing, so we stopped at the makeshift salesrooms established by the Emporium, the largest department store in the city, and were lucky enough to find a jacket and a pair of knickerbockers that fit me fairly well. If I remember correctly, the outfit cost twelve dollars. After that we stopped briefly to call on some family friends who lived on Franklin Street, just a few yards from the western limit of the burned area. Eventually we joined my mother at our Pacific Avenue house, and were driven (I do not remember in what vehicle) back to the Ferry Building, where we deposited our luggage. My mother and I returned to San Rafael, and we did not go to the city again until the morning of our departure for New York, and then only as far as the Ferry Building, where we took the ferryboat to the Oakland Mole, the terminus of

1906

~~

the transcontinental railroad. (The Bay Bridge and Golden Gate Bridge were not built until thirty years later.) My father accompanied us to Oakland, where my mother and I boarded the Overland Limited.

During all of the following summer my father lived, or rather camped out, in the Pacific Avenue house, attended only by the Chinese laundryman. Until electricity and gas were reconnected, candles supplied the only light at night. There was no running water, so they dug an earth closet, enclosed in a ramshackle screen of boards, in the back yard. Until the kitchen chimney had been inspected and repaired, all cooking was done on a small stove set on a few bricks on the sidewalk, similar to thousands of outdoor stoves in front of almost all the habitable houses in the city. One hydrant, three or four blocks from the house and down a very steep hill, was in working order. Twice a day my father and the laundryman would trudge down to the hydrant and carry heavy pails of water uphill to the house. That was all the water they had for drinking (boiled), cooking, keeping themselves moderately clean, and washing a minimum of laundry, until the water mains were repaired some months later. Years afterwards my father suddenly remembered that when the new house was built he had insisted on having a large tank of fresh water installed on the roof, for use in an emergency. But when the emergency occurred he forgot all about the tank; and there it sat unused, while he and the laundryman toiled up the hills with their heavy water pails. The tank would not have supplied their needs for very long, but it certainly would have saved many back-breaking water-laden climbs, if only my father had remembered in time that it existed.

By the time my mother and I returned to San Francisco in November, seven months after the earthquake, the house was once more in perfect order. Electric lights, gas, telephones, and the water system were working normally; the big front chimney was being rebuilt and anchored to the

18

1906

house more firmly than before; the two interior chimneys, including the one serving the kitchen, were repaired; the earth closet had been removed; and the sidewalk stove had disappeared. Most of the streetcar lines were running (though many of the obsolete cable systems had been replaced by more efficient electric cars), and life in general returned to normal except that for the next three years Van Ness Avenue remained the principal shopping street while the entire burned area to the east was being rebuilt.

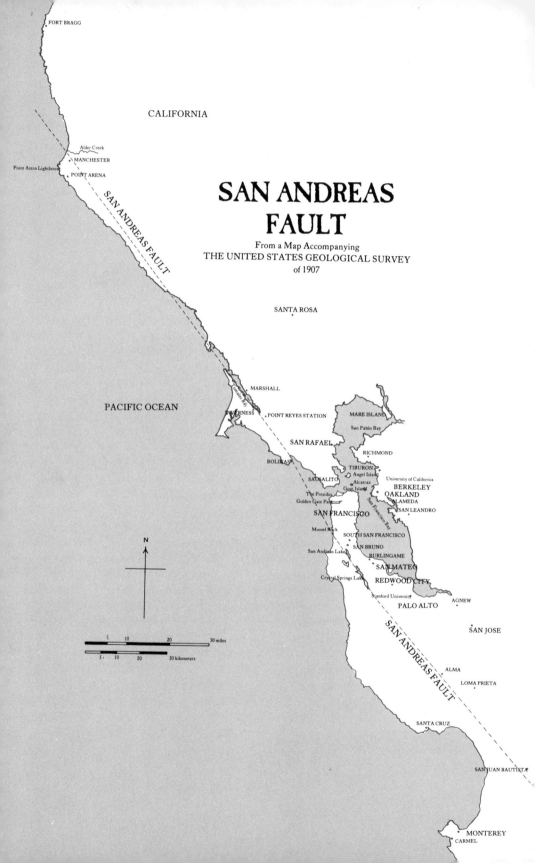

FORT BRAGG

CALIFORNIA

Alder Creek
MANCHESTER
Point Arena Lighthouse
POINT ARENA

SAN ANDREAS FAULT

SAN ANDREAS
FAULT

From a Map Accompanying
THE UNITED STATES GEOLOGICAL SURVEY
of 1907

SANTA ROSA

PACIFIC OCEAN

MARSHALL
Tomales Bay
INVERNESS
POINT REYES STATION

MARE ISLAND
San Pablo Bay

SAN RAFAEL

RICHMOND

BOLINAS

TIBURON
Angel Island
SAUSALITO
Alcatraz
Goat Island
The Presidio
Golden Gate Park

University of California
BERKELEY
OAKLAND
ALAMEDA
SAN LEANDRO

SAN FRANCISCO

San Francisco Bay

Mussel Rock
San Andreas Lake
Crystal Springs Lake

SOUTH SAN FRANCISCO
SAN BRUNO
BURLINGAME
SAN MATEO
REDWOOD CITY

N

Stanford University
PALO ALTO

AGNEW

SAN JOSE

5   10   20   30 miles
5   10   20   30 kilometers

SAN ANDREAS FAULT

ALMA
LOMA PRIETA

SANTA CRUZ

SAN JUAN BAUTISTA

MONTEREY
CARMEL

LEGEND

1 ALTA PLAZA
2 APPRAISERS' BUILDING
3 CHRONICLE BUILDING
4 CITY HALL
5 CROCKER BUILDING
6 CROCKER RESIDENCE
7 CUSTOM HOUSE
8 EMPORIUM
9 FAIRMONT HOTEL
10 FERRY BUILDING
11 FLOOD BUILDING
12 FLOOD RESIDENCE
13 FRANKLIN SQUARE
14 GRAND OPERA HOUSE
15 "HAM AND EGG" FIRE STARTED HERE
16 HEARST BUILDING
17 HOPKINS RESIDENCE
18 HUNTINGTON RESIDENCE
19 JEFFERSON SQUARE
20 KOHL BUILDING
21 LAFAYETTE SQUARE
22 MECHANICS' PAVILION
23 MERCHANTS' EXCHANGE
24 MINT
25 MISSION DOLORES
26 MONTGOMERY BLOCK
27 PALACE HOTEL
28 PHELAN BUILDING
29 PORTSMITH SQUARE
30 POST OFFICE
31 ST. FRANCIS HOTEL
32 SOUTHERN PACIFIC RAILROAD
     STATION
33 SPRECKELS (CALL) BUILDING
34 SPRECKELS RESIDENCE
35 STANFORD RESIDENCE
36 TOWNE RESIDENCE
37 UNION SQUARE
38 VALENCIA STREET HOTEL

BURNED AREA

PART OF
SAN FRANCISCO
From a Map Accompanying
THE UNITED STATES GEOLOGICAL SURVEY
of 1907

1906

According to the seismograph in the observatory of the University of California at Berkeley, the earth began to shake at twelve minutes and six seconds after five o'clock on Wednesday morning, April 18. The earthquake lasted sixty-five seconds—a very long time as earthquakes go—and during the entire period the vibrations were extremely violent and fantastically complex: horizontal, vertical, wavelike, and rotary motions all churned the ground simultaneously. The corkscrew twistings produced very curious effects: heavy pieces of furniture slid in all directions and turned in half circles; pictures suspended on long cords or wires swung out from the walls and slammed back again with their faces against the plaster. Most earthquakes are accompanied by more or less audible rumblings, and these were heard (or at any rate were reported later) by many people in San Francisco; but for most of the inhabitants such subterranean sounds were smothered by the much louder noises of toppling chimneys, rattling windows, creaking woodwork, and the crashing and shattering of china, glass, and bric-a-brac. At that hour, of course, almost everyone was still in bed, and a few exceptionally sound sleepers managed, almost incredibly, to slumber through the terrific shaking. Many of those who, suddenly awakened, tried to get up were knocked

1906

〰

off their feet and sprawled on the heaving floors. But as soon as the earthquake stopped, people poured out of their houses, some in their night clothes, others half dressed, and a few—more modest or perhaps merely more phlegmatic—fully attired. Almost everybody was frightened to some extent, but there was very little actual panic.

Modern theories of continental drift assume that the lithosphere or hard outer layer of the earth's surface is divided into a number of plates about sixty miles thick, resting upon beds of softer material. These plates are in almost constant but very slow motion, gradually altering the shapes and relative positions of continents and oceans as they slide towards or away from each other. One of the longest and most nearly continuous lines of collision extends along the entire west coast of North, Central, and South America, where the great continental plates, moving westward, meet the Pacific plate underlying almost all of that immense ocean. The boundaries of these plates, on both the American and Asian sides of the Pacific, are the sites of numerous volcanoes and frequent earthquakes.

The San Andreas fault in California is a fracture of the earth's crust that marks a section of the boundary between two great plates. The Pacific plate west of the fault is moving northwest in relation to the adjacent North American plate. The fracture was probably formed about thirty million years ago, and it is believed that during this period the displacement between the two sides of the fault was about 350 miles, approximately the distance in a straight line between San Francisco and Los Angeles.

The San Andreas is the longest and most important of a group of more or less parallel fractures at varying distances from the main rift. The northern end of this fault lies under the ocean; its precise location is unknown. It enters the land near the mouth of Alder Creek, a rivulet just north of Point Arena in Mendocino County, where the earthquake de-

23

1906

molished a wooden bridge. Thence it runs south-southeast in an almost straight line for about two hundred miles to San Juan Bautista in San Benito County, passing close to and approximately parallel with the shore, partly on land and partly under the sea. Southeast of San Juan the rift continues for several hundred miles, but in this section the surface of the ground was not disturbed and no buildings were damaged, though the shock was violent and there may have been some displacement of the underlying rock. Along the plane of cleavage the ground shifted horizontally, the land west of the fault moving northwest, that on the east side to the southeast. North of San Francisco the horizontal displacement amounted in several areas to sixteen feet, and in a few instances to twenty-one feet. South of the city the ground shifted only six to eight feet. The vertical dislocation was much smaller, varying from a few inches to four feet. All the way from Point Arena to San Juan Bautista the land surface along the fault was violently churned up throughout a belt or zone from fifty feet to a quarter of a mile wide. In places the ground split open and formed deep fissures, in other places it was squeezed together into ridges, and in some areas the soil was broken and furrowed as if by a gigantic plow. Enormous oaks were uprooted, and the trunks of sequoias four or five feet in diameter were ruptured vertically, the two halves slipping past each other like wooden blocks.

Practically every man-made structure situated directly on or very close to the fault line was either severely damaged or totally destroyed. Culverts and water pipes snapped in two, trestles and bridges shifted on their piers and abutments. Roads that had originally run straight across the fault were twisted into S-shaped curves. Every fence that crossed the rift was sliced off as if by a sharp knife, with the severed ends separated by many feet. A large section of the town of Fort Bragg, more than thirty miles north of Alder Creek, collapsed in heaps of rubble. The solid masonry lighthouse at

The train at Point Reyes Station.

Point Arena was wrecked, as were most of the houses in that community and in nearby Manchester. Farther south, in the Tomales Bay area, where the fault runs under the sea for several miles, railroad tracks were torn up; a small summer hotel at Marshall was thrown bodily into the bay, where it landed right side up, the boarders bewildered but unhurt; three cottages at Inverness and the Flagstaff Inn at Bolinas fell into the sea and were completely demolished. At Point Reyes Station the early morning train for San Francisco was on the point of departure, and the conductor had just climbed aboard, when the cars gave a lurch and the whole train toppled over on its side.

Even the surface of the Pacific Ocean felt the effects of the earthquake along the submarine sections of the fault. Off Cape Mendocino, more than ninety miles north of Point Arena, a small steamer, the *Argo,* was suddenly tossed about in a choppy sea which had been perfectly calm a moment before; so violent was the shock of the waves that the captain thought the ship had struck a raft of logs or some similar obstruction. A fisherman reported that the waters of Tomales

1906

~~

Bay abruptly receded, leaving his boat high and dry on the mud, and then swept back in a huge wave "which looked a hundred feet high, but which was probably no more than ten."[1]

Earthquakes are often followed by tsunamis, commonly called tidal waves, which frequently cause more loss of life and damage to property than the quakes themselves. The earthquake of 1755 at Lisbon, for example, was succeeded by such a wave, which added greatly to the destruction of the city. Tsunamis travel at speeds of 350 to 450 miles an hour, and waves one hundred feet in height have been recorded. Fortunately no such disaster accompanied the California earthquake of 1906. The rise of a few feet in the water level of Tomales Bay was not duplicated anywhere else along the coast. The tidal gauge at the Presidio registered a negligible rise of six inches in the level of San Francisco Bay, which quickly returned to normal.

Santa Rosa, nineteen miles east of the San Andreas fault, suffered more severely in proportion to its area and population than any community in the state, not excepting San Francisco itself. There were three reasons for the unparalleled amount of destruction. The town is situated near a secondary fault that runs approximately in the same direction as the great rift, and it is probable that a local break occurred at the same time as the main fracture; it rests on relatively soft soil; and the business district, built amost entirely of brick, "had been put together with a lime mortar made of poor sand. Little attention had been paid to the need for adequate cross bracing, cross walls, and proper anchoring of walls to floor and roof."[2] The devastation was completed by a conflagration with which the inadequately equipped firemen were unable to cope. Santa Rosa was the only city except San Francisco in which the earthquake was followed by a disastrous fire. Estimates of the number of dead varied between sixty-four and seventy-five.

The Santa Rosa Courthouse.

No large town is located directly on the San Andreas fault. At Bolinas the rift again dips into the ocean and continues its southeasterly course, passing six or seven miles west of the Golden Gate and three to five miles from the western shore of San Francisco, a section of the city which at that time consisted largely of sand dunes and was sparsely inhabited. At no point does the fault run within the city limits. It re-enters the land near Mussel Rock, about three miles south of the line between San Francisco and San Mateo counties, where the shock waves caused a landslide that swept four thousand feet of the unfinished roadbed of the Ocean Shore Railroad into the sea. It cuts through the narrow San Andreas Valley, which gives the fault its name, and through the San Andreas and Crystal Springs reservoirs and their massive dams of reinforced concrete. These dams, scientifically designed and sturdily built of the best materials, were the only artificial structures situated precisely on the rift that remained intact; the earth abutments were slightly damaged but no leaks occurred. Burlingame and San Mateo, though only some three or four miles from the fault, escaped with

27

The library at Stanford University.

relatively slight injury; but at Redwood City, Stanford University, and San Jose the destruction was appalling. In Redwood City the new courthouse and a number of other structures were almost totally wrecked. Nearly all of the stone buildings on the Stanford campus were more or less seriously damaged: immense chunks of debris from the topheavy memorial arch and the mosaic facade of the chapel littered the ground, the new library and gymnasium had crumbled into shapeless ruins, and in one of the dormitories, Encina Hall, the chimneys had crashed through the roof and floors, killing one student and injuring several others. One of the maintenance men on the campus was also killed.

One reason for the vast amount of damage in Redwood City, Palo Alto (including the Stanford campus), and San Jose was the softness of the ground. In the city of San Jose, thirteen miles east of the San Andreas fault, most of the stone and brick public buildings, schoolhouses, and churches were demolished, and several inadequately braced wooden structures—notably the annex to the Hotel Vendome—collapsed. In San Jose twenty-four people died and ten were

The annex of the Hotel Vendome in San Jose.

gravely injured. The state insane asylum at Agnew, six miles north of San Jose, was almost literally shaken to pieces. The huge brick administration building and all of the twenty smaller buildings were shattered so completely that not one remained in habitable condition. The United States Geological Survey of 1907 condemned the construction of this institution in the harshest terms: "Perhaps the worst example of poor design, bad workmanship, and poor materials in the earthquake territory, except in the city of San Francisco, is the insane asylum at Agnew. . . ." The buildings were "all flimsily constructed brick structures with timber frames. The construction of these buildings, with their thin walls (in many places devoid of mortar) and light, insufficient wood framing, indicates a criminal negligence that is appalling."[3] One hundred seventeen patients and attendants (some reports say 119) lost their lives here, most of them crushed to death when the central tower of the main building collapsed. The surviving inmates and staff, numbering nearly one thousand, were temporarily housed in tents and in hurriedly constructed shacks. Some of the more violent patients were tied to trees to keep

The State Insane Asylum at Agnew.

them from injuring themselves and others. "During the disaster," the San Francisco *Chronicle* reported two weeks later, "many patients considered hopelessly insane worked with all the intelligence and vigor that were exhibited by the attendants. . . . One young woman is known to have saved the lives of at least three or four persons, yet after it was all over the great darkness came again upon her, and she understood nothing of what she had done."[4]

Where the fault crosses the Santa Cruz Mountains an avalanche completely buried the Loma Prieta sawmill, located at the bottom of a deep narrow gorge, and killed nine of the mill workmen. The southernmost point of destruction was the historic mission of San Juan Bautista, founded in 1797, which was reduced to rubble. The old crumbled adobe from the side walls of the mission church, the largest in California, has been recycled and made into new bricks of the same size and shape as the originals, and the entire group of mission buildings has been reconstructed; but restoration was a slow process and was not completed until 1976, seventy years after the earthquake. The seaside towns of Santa Cruz, Monterey,

1906

~~

and Carmel were practically uninjured. In the enormous
Hotel Del Monte near Monterey a few chimneys fell, and it
was reported that two guests, a young Texan and his bride on
their honeymoon, were killed. The cities on the eastern shore
of San Francisco Bay, though violently shaken, were built on
rock or firm ground and suffered only relatively minor damage. In Oakland several walls and a good many chimneys collapsed, and five people were crushed to death in the ruins of
the Empire Theater. The dilapidation in Berkeley was
almost wholly confined to cracked and fallen chimneys, and
none of the buildings on the University of California campus
were injured. The most remarkable phenomenon in the entire
earthquake zone was reported from the rock island of Alcatraz, site of the famous Federal penitentiary, located in the
bay only about a mile from San Francisco. On this island, it
was said, the shock was not felt at all!

San Franciscans are notoriously reluctant, even now, to refer
to the disaster as "the earthquake." They prefer to call it "the
fire," and frequently date events as having taken place "before
the fire" or "after the fire," almost never before or after "the
earthquake." This sensitivity is apparently based on the as-
sumption that a conflagration may occur anywhere at any
time, whereas there is something vaguely invidious about an
earthquake, some local or regional menace that might, if
talked about too openly, give the city a bad name and frighten
away visitors and prospective residents. But the inhabitants
of San Francisco are more likely to justify their tendency to
emphasize the fire and slur over the earthquake by pointing
out, quite truthfully, that the fire accounted for ninety percent
of the destruction, and that although the earthquake was the
direct cause of the fire, the damage wrought by the quake
alone within the city was of no great importance and could
have been repaired, with a very few exceptions, within two or
three months.

1906

The extent of earthquake damage in different sections of San Francisco, as in all the communities affected, depended chiefly upon two factors: the nature of the ground and the type and quality of construction. Buildings erected on the solid rock of the steep slopes and the hilltops suffered least. Those on the fairly firm soil of the valleys between the heights were somewhat more seriously injured; on the rolling sand dunes the damage was still more apparent; and the greatest destruction occurred in the artificially filled area near the bay and especially in sections of the district south of Market Street overlying an old swamp and the loosely filled-in bed of Mission Creek. On the landfill close to the waterfront some of the street surfaces sank several feet, and in places the pavements were distorted into waves and hummocks. Worst of all was the devastation on the marshy ground in the vicinity of 19th and Valencia streets. Here the soggy soil shook like jelly; streets were torn up and cracked in all directions; streetcar tracks were twisted into fantastic curves; several wooden houses, precariously supported on little more than stilts, settled at crazy angles or collapsed in heaps of kindling; and the four-story wooden Valencia Street Hotel, one of the city's many unpretentious hostelries, sank into the soft ground until its top floor touched the street level, crushing and burying the tenants in the rooms below. The number of deaths in this hotel has been estimated at twenty to thirty-five, but the precise figure was never established because the fire consumed the whole district before the wrecked building could be searched.

But even on spongy land, well-constructed buildings on properly designed foundations survived the shock. The Ferry Building at the foot of Market Street, terminus of all transbay passenger traffic, built on landfill and resting on a foundation of wooden piles, remained structurally intact, though the stone facing of its lofty slender tower, loosened by the swaying, had to be taken down and replaced. Similarly

The Valencia Street Hotel near Nineteenth Street.

the sturdy main Federal Post office, located on a poorly chosen site directly over an arm of what had once been Mission Creek, suffered only superficial damage to its exterior stonework, although the adjacent streets and sidewalks buckled and subsided, exposing part of the foundation.

Throughout the city the violent wrenching and twisting had little effect on scientifically designed buildings constructed of good materials. Practically all of the steel-framed office structures, including the tallest skyscraper in San Francisco at that time—the twenty-story Spreckels Building, usually known as the Call Building—were unharmed by the quake. There were then no buildings in the city constructed wholly of reinforced concrete, but the absence of any injury to floors and interior walls of this material indicated that reinforced concrete could safely be used in the future. Structures with wooden frames, comprising most of the smaller business buildings and almost all of the residences, also stood up well if their foundations were sound and the frames, roofs, and exterior walls were firmly tied together. All of these types of construction possessed one essential qual-

The San Francisco City Hall.

ity that enabled them to resist the stresses produced by an earthquake: resilience. Framed buildings, of either steel or wood, could sway and vibrate freely while the jolting continued and then return unharmed to their original positions. On the other hand, ordinary brick or stone buildings with self- supporting walls unattached or inadequately attached to interior frames were too rigid to "give," and such structures, unless they were exceptionally well built, were all severely injured. For the same reason thousands of brick chimneys all over the city cracked and toppled.

The only very large and important building that was completely wrecked by the earthquake was the City Hall, which had cost the taxpayers almost seven million dollars and had taken seventeen years to build. Poorly designed and carelessly constructed of shoddy materials by contractors who, with the connivance of dishonest municipal officials, ignored

1906

the architectural specifications, this huge structure simply fell apart. Tons of masonry from the ornate topheavy cornices crashed into the streets, and most of the massive sheathing of the cylindrical tower, decorated with tiers of columns which actually supported nothing, dropped away, leaving the great metal dome perched high in the air on its naked steel frame. Hours before the flames reached the City Hall and destroyed what the earthquake had left of it, this "monument of graft and incompetence" had fallen into grim unsightly ruin.[5]

The Richter scale, now in general use as a measure of the amount of energy released at the focus of an earthquake, was not devised by Charles F. Richter until 1935, many years after the California quake of 1906. It is a logarithmic scale on which each whole number represents a magnitude ten times as great as the preceding whole number. Thus an earthquake that registers 8 on the Richter scale is ten times as severe as one marked 7, one hundred times as powerful as one of a magnitude of 6, one thousand times as violent as one marked 5, and so forth. Estimates of the magnitude of the 1906 earthquake range from 7.8 to 8.3, amply sufficient to rank it among the great earthquakes of history. The shock waves were felt distinctly in southern California and in parts of Nevada and Oregon, hundreds of miles from the center of disturbance, and were registered by seismographs in countries as distant as Germany and Japan. For many weeks after the first violent quake, numerous minor shocks of varying intensity occurred at irregular intervals as the earth near the plane of rupture settled and readjusted itself. There was some fear in San Francisco that another earthquake as intense as the first might follow at any moment, but this anxiety was unwarranted. Once a major rupture and slippage of the rock have taken place, the stresses that caused them are relieved, and there is little danger that another break will occur until, after several years, new irresistible strains produce a new fracture along the line of an old fault.

1906

W̶ithin fifteen minutes after the earthquake, ominous columns of smoke could
be seen rising in different parts of the
city. The fires started in various ways:
stoves were lighted in houses whose owners were unaware
that their chimneys had cracked, and sparks set the roofs
ablaze; gas exploded in mains broken by the earthquake;
electric connections were damaged, causing short circuits;
high-tension wires snapped and fell across shingled roofs.
Eyewitness accounts vary so greatly that the precise number
of "original" fires is uncertain, but there were at least a dozen,
perhaps twenty. Less than an hour later more than fifty buildings were aflame. Most of these were in the district south of
Market Street, where several separate fires soon merged into
a conflagration with its center in the vicinity of Third and
Mission streets. The fire department was efficient and well
equipped, but the firemen were handicapped at first by the
scattered locations of the burning buildings, which obliged
them to dissipate their efforts over a wide area. In a very short
time another and infinitely more serious difficulty became apparent: there was no water. The streams from the hoses
diminished to mere trickles, then stopped altogether. A few
roof tanks, underground cisterns, artesian wells, and small
local reservoirs continued to supply water, and in some flat
sections of the city water was pumped from sewers; but the
earthquake had broken most of the mains within the city as
well as the big conduits leading from the great reservoirs outside. The firemen were almost helpless.

At that time, before the construction of the present
Hetch Hetchy reservoir in the Sierras, San Francisco derived
its water supply from four sources: the San Andreas, Crystal
Springs, and Pilarcitos lakes south of the city, and one or two

1906

reservoirs in Alameda County across the bay. The conduit running under the bay from the east was undamaged, but breaks in the pipes on shore at Dumbarton Point put this system out of commission. The Crystal Springs conduit, partly laid in very soft ground, was wrenched and fractured in many places, the worst destruction occurring where the line crossed a salt marsh on a trestle between San Bruno and South San Francisco. From Pilarcitos the path of the conduit coincided for about six miles with the actual line of the great fault; throughout this section the pipes were torn apart violently at a number of points, as violently telescoped at others. The San Andreas pipeline, passing through fairly solid ground approximately midway between the fault and the marsh, suffered relatively slight damage and was repaired within three days after the earthquake—too late to save the city from the flames but in time to avert a serious water famine. For several weeks this reservoir supplied all the water that flowed into San Francisco. Within the city limits smaller storage reservoirs held about eighty million gallons, but although these reservoirs remained intact the water could not be distributed because many of the mains and branch pipes, especially those laid in soft earth, were broken, and the system lacked bypasses through which water might have been detoured.

Early in the morning a series of scattered fires near the waterfront quickly combined into another center of conflagration. East Street (now called the Embarcadero), a very broad curving thoroughfare separating the city from the docks that jutted into the bay, was flanked on its west or city side by rows of old wooden buildings housing the tawdry establishments common to all seaports: ship chandleries, drab restaurants and saloons, frowzy hotels and boarding houses catering to sailors, "cheap John" secondhand clothing shops. The flames consumed these rattletraps like tinder and swept on through the adjacent factory district, more substantially constructed but not much more resistant to the intense heat of the

1906

~~

blaze. At first there seemed to be a faint chance that the great width of Market Street, the main thoroughfare of the city, might suffice to confine the conflagration to the southern areas, but this hope quickly faded. The ramshackle wooden buildings on East Street north of Market, similar to those a little farther south, soon caught fire. From these the flames spread westward through the wholesale district and north towards the Latin Quarter at the foot of Telegraph Hill.

About ten in the morning a new fire started independently near the corner of Gough and Hayes streets, in a middle-class residential section known as Hayes Valley not far from the present Civic Center, and advanced eastward across Van Ness Avenue to sweep through the already ruined City Hall. This blaze was nicknamed the "ham-and-egg" fire because it was said to have been started by a woman who, not realizing that her chimney was cracked, cooked herself a breakfast of ham and eggs and set fire to her kitchen wall and her roof. Meanwhile the flames drove swiftly along Mission Street, roared through the Grand Opera House, and attacked the great office buildings, stores, and hotels on the south side of Market Street. At the corner of Third and Market the tall Spreckels Building, home of the San Francisco *Call,* burst into a tower of flame, and across Third Street the Hearst Building, headquarters of the *Examiner,* quickly burned to the ground. Farther west on Market Street the Emporium, the largest department store on the Pacific Coast, blazed furiously with all its combustible stock, leaving only the stone facade upright. By noon, seven hours after the earthquake, about one square mile of the city was in ashes.

That morning the weather was warm and sunny, and the air was unusually still for San Francisco. "Earthquake weather," many people called it, and the belief in "earthquake weather" still persists. Actually it is pure superstition;

Opposite: The Call, or Spreckels Building at Market and Third streets.

1906

earthquakes can, and do, occur in any sort of weather, at any time of the day or night, and at any season of the year. During the afternoon a light westerly breeze sprang up, too gentle to produce any perceptible effect on the progress of the fire.

For several hours the famous Palace Hotel, considered the most luxurious in the world when it was opened in 1875, withstood the conflagration that was closing in from three sides. The hotel, covering an entire block on the south side of Market Street, had its own reservoir supplied by an artesian well. In a desperate effort to save the huge structure, two attempts were made to dynamite the unfinished Monadnock Building standing between the hotel and the already blazing Hearst Building. Both were unsuccessful; the explosive charges were too weak to make any impression on the solidly constructed office building, and early that afternoon it was gutted by the fire. By that time the reservoir under the Palace had gone dry, and soon tongues of flame were shooting from hundreds of bay windows. Before dusk nothing was left of the great hotel but the roofless walls.

The efforts of the fire fighters to stop or at least control the conflagration were hampered not only by lack of water but also by a tragic accident: the injury and subsequent death of Fire Chief Dennis T. Sullivan. It was generally believed that Sullivan, who had been connected with the San Francisco Fire Department for twenty-nine years and the head of it for fourteen, had worked out a comprehensive plan for just such an emergency, including the possibility of a failure of the water supply. Presumably this program involved the widespread use of dynamite and "backfiring" (the deliberate burning of buildings to create an empty zone which the main conflagration could not cross). Whatever his plan might have been—if in truth it did actually exist in his mind—the chief apparently failed to communicate it to his subordinates; but even if there had been no such plan, the chief's disability undoubtedly deprived the department of valuable qualities of

The Palace Hotel burning.

leadership and discipline. At the time of the first earthquake shock, Sullivan and his wife were sleeping in adjoining rooms in the firehouse of Engine Company No. 3 on Bush Street, next door to the California Hotel. A turret of the hotel fell through the ceiling of Mrs. Sullivan's room, slightly injuring her and carrying away a section of the floor. Sullivan ran into his wife's room and, half blinded by the cloud of mortar dust, plunged through the broken floor, followed by a cascade of bricks. He landed heavily on a heap of debris, breaking two ribs, puncturing a lung, injuring his head, and severely scalding himself by being thrown against the hot pipes of a radiator. Mrs. Sullivan, who was also hurled through the jagged opening, saved herself from serious harm by rolling herself in her mattress just as the floor gave way. The chief was rushed to the Receiving Hospital in the City Hall, but the building was so badly damaged that his attendants drove him to the Railroad Hospital. Later in the day he was moved to the military hospital at the Presidio, where he died very early Sunday morning, four days after the earthquake. He remained conscious almost to the end, but was told nothing about the fire

The gutted St. Francis Hotel, with its new wing under construction.

and died without knowing that the department in which he took such pride had failed to prevent a catastrophe.

Throughout Wednesday night the fire advanced steadily on two fronts. One conflagration spread south and west through block after block of modest wooden dwellings in the Mission district. The other blaze, north of Market Street, gutted the Crocker Building; the Chronicle Building with its new seventeen-story annex; the Flood Building; and many other large office structures, as completely as their counterparts across the street had been burned out a few hours earlier. The financial district on Sansome and Montgomery streets, catching fire from the wholesale section farther east, blazed fiercely. The entire retail district with its fine shops, many of them founded in pioneer days, was destroyed in a few hours. All of the buildings facing Union Square, including the new St. Francis Hotel, of which two wings were occupied and a third was under construction, were either gutted or burned to the ground.

1906

As the fire climbed the steep eastern slope of Nob Hill it licked up the flimsy and insanitary but picturesque buildings in crowded Chinatown. By dawn on Thursday, twenty-four hours after the earthquake, the flames were approaching the crest of the hill. During the morning they continued their westward progress, more slowly now because the great mansions on top of Nob Hill were widely spaced and surrounded by extensive lawns and gardens. One by one the ornate wooden houses on California Street belonging to the families of the "Big Four" of the Central Pacific Railroad—Leland Stanford, Mark Hopkins, Collis P. Huntington, and Charles Crocker—crumbled to ashes. Only a roofless rectangle of brownstone walls remained of the James Flood house. The Fairmont Hotel, then under construction and about six months short of completion, contained little that was inflammable; the flames roared through the empty shell, blackening the cream-colored terra cotta facing and destroying such wooden fittings as had already been installed, but causing little damage to the structure itself.

During the last twenty-four hours there had been a number of attempts to halt the conflagration by dynamiting buildings in various parts of the city, but the firemen, inexperienced in the use of explosives, hesitated to demolish areas sufficiently broad and continuous to check the flames, and their timid efforts were ineffectual. Moreover, the supply of dynamite on hand was limited. Early on Wednesday morning the acting fire chief sent a request to the military post at the Presidio for all available explosives and for a detail of troops to handle them. Three hundred pounds of dynamite and several barrels of artillery powder were sent at once; a little later, larger amounts of dynamite were obtained from the California Powder works (which afterwards refused to accept any payment for this contribution); and a small quantity of gun-

Overleaf: View of the burning city from Lafayette Square.

43

1906

~~

cotton arrived from the naval base at Mare Island. On Thursday afternoon a westerly breeze again started to blow, this time briskly enough to reduce the speed of the fire's advance to about half a block an hour. As the flames crept slowly down the western slope of Nob Hill the fire fighters decided to make one last desperate attempt to save the Western Addition, the principal residence district of the city, by boldly dynamiting and backfiring all the buildings—mostly dignified old-fashioned wooden dwellings—on the east side of Van Ness Avenue, in the hope that the space thus cleared, plus the great width of the avenue itself, would stop the westward progress of the fire. The charges were set by the firemen, detachments of soldiers from the Presidio, and volunteers; fuses were lighted, and row after row of fine houses blew up with a deafening roar. Other houses along the avenue were sprayed with kerosene and backfired, and field guns battered down all walls and fragments of walls left standing after the blasting and burning had done their work.

This belated campaign of deliberate ruthless demolition was, to a very great extent, successful. The fire was checked on the eastern side of Van Ness Avenue except in the five blocks between Clay and Sutter streets, where it crossed the broad thoroughfare, consumed all of the houses on the opposite side (including the magnificent red sandstone residence of Claus Spreckels), and swept one block farther west to Franklin Street. Here, with the aid of salt water pumped from the bay through hoses a mile long, and with the additional assistance of the west wind, the exhausted fire fighters finally succeeded in extinguishing the flames at about two o'clock on Friday morning, forty-five hours after the start of the conflagration. At approximately the same hour, the fire in the Mission district was halted near 20th Street on the east side of Dolores, a street as wide as Van Ness Avenue and an even more effective barrier to the flames. The Western Addition and the more remote, more thinly populated residence

View of the burning city from Russian Hill.

areas beyond, extending westward to the ocean, were safe, as were all of the poorer sections of the city south of 20th Street, and the Potrero district with its iron foundries and other heavy industries.

But the fire, stopped on three sides, still blazed fiercely on the fourth. The flames sweeping over Nob Hill had remained south of Washington Street until Thursday afternoon, when they jumped across the narrow street and spread rapidly to the north. Fanned by the west wind which had helped to slow down and finally to extinguish the main conflagration, the new blaze advanced in the opposite direction—eastward—and climbed the western slope of Russian Hill, then over the crown and down the other side into the thickly settled valley of the Latin Quarter, and up Telegraph Hill. The inhabitants of the North Beach district, caught between the fire and the bay, were rescued by tugs and steam schooners. A few houses on top of Russian Hill were saved by their owners, assisted by neighbors, who filled bathtubs and other receptacles with water drawn from a small local reservoir and, for seven hot and weary hours, stubbornly beat out the

Sacramento Street looking east from Nob Hill.

flames with wet blankets. Their strenuous efforts were considerably hampered by what the *Chronicle* called "the almost
irrepressible desire of the dynamiters to blow up the entire
row."[6] On Telegraph Hill several houses were preserved by
similar methods, but here there was little or no water, so the
inhabitants, most of whom were of Italian birth or descent,
soaked their blankets in casks of wine.

All day Friday and on Friday night the fire raged over
Russian and Telegraph hills and through North Beach. By
Saturday morning it had reached the bay, had swept through
the lumber yards and iron foundries located at the foot of the
hills, and was threatening Pier 27, the northernmost of all the
docks. Here the worn-out fire fighters made a final stand.
Dousing the pier with salt water from the bay, they quenched
the last blaze in this area. By mid-afternoon on Saturday,
April 21—three and a half days after the earthquake—the fire
was out. For more than three weeks, coal dumps in the indus-
trial district south of Market Street continued to burn, and
piles of coffee and tea in a warehouse smoldered, emitting a
rich aroma; but these half-smothered embers were no longer

1906

〜

sources of danger, because everything else in their vicinity had already been destroyed.

The fire was out; but most of the city was in ruins. The area of the burned district covered 2,593 acres—a little more than four square miles—comprising 490 city blocks and parts of 32 others. The flames had devoured 28,188 buildings, and the irregular perimeter of the ruined section measured more than eleven miles in length. The area of destruction was eighteen times that caused by the Baltimore fire of 1904, eight times as great as that of the famous fire of London in 1666, and one-fourth larger than the area of the Chicago fire of 1871. In San Francisco the property loss was estimated at about five hundred million dollars, or $1,100 per capita. In terms of dollars and cents it was by far the greatest disaster that had ever befallen a single city. All of the wholesale, retail, and financial areas were destroyed. Every good hotel was gone, and most of the cheaper ones had vanished as well. Not a theater or restaurant was left. Practically every store larger than a neighborhood grocery was in ashes. The municipality of San Francisco, which was conterminous with San Francisco County, sustained very heavy losses. The City Hall, the Hall of Records, the Hall of Justice, the county jail, the public library (housed in a wing of the City Hall), thirteen fire engine houses, and numerous police stations were burned. Twenty-nine public schools were totally wrecked by the fire, and many others, constructed—as the City Hall had been—by incompetent or dishonest contractors, were severely damaged by the earthquake.

Added to the financial loss was the destruction of irreplaceable records. All certificates of births, marriages, and deaths were burned. Of more than fourteen hundred thick volumes of mortgage registrations in the Hall of Records, only a single volume was salvaged. Three-fifths of the property deeds went up in smoke. On the other hand, quick-

Nob Hill from Broadway near Kearny. The ruins of Chinatown are in left center. On the summit are the unfinished Fairmont Hotel and the roofless stone walls of the James Flood Mansion.

witted and courageous employees carried away and preserved many valuable documents: the tax rolls, the papers and photographs of the police department, and the ancient records, priceless to historians, of the days of Spanish and Mexican sovereignty. Damage to powerhouses and transmission lines had put out of commission all electric lights, telephones, telegraph wires, and streetcars (at that time mostly cable-cars) in the city. There was no gas; the earthquake had broken the mains. The city had little water and less food. About two hundred thousand people—almost half the total population—were homeless.

And yet, as the immense clouds of smoke drifted away, they exposed a few scattered patches of silver lining. All of the docks, extending along the bay front for more than two miles, were saved, as were the Ferry Building and the ferry slips. The waterfront, menaced by flying sparks and embers during every minute of the three-day conflagration, owed its ultimate escape to two factors: the enormous breadth of

1906

~~

East Street separating the wharves from the burning city, and the unremitting efforts of the fire fighters. Two fire boats sent from the Mare Island Navy Yard kept the wooden piers drenched with salt water, while fire engines sprayed the sheds from the land side. In order to maintain a supply of fresh water for the boilers of these engines, a boat constantly shuttled back and forth between the city and Goat Island (now Yerba Buena Island) in the middle of the bay. The preservation of the docks and ferry slips was of vital importance. San Francisco, situated between the bay and the ocean at the northern tip of a peninsula forty miles long, is surrounded on three sides by water. Before the great bridges across the bay and the Golden Gate were built, thirty years after the fire, nine-tenths of the passenger traffic and much of the freight transport between San Francisco and its neighbors was water-borne. The earthquake had seriously damaged the single railroad line to the south. If the waterfront had been destroyed the city would have been completely cut off from the outside world, and thousands—perhaps hundreds of thousands—of its inhabitants might have starved to death.

In addition to the piers, a few other important structures survived. The fire stopped just before it reached the only railroad station in the city, the Southern Pacific depot at Third and Townsend streets. The wooden building was saved chiefly by the exertions of three energetic men who, with nothing but an ordinary garden hose and a very thin trickle of water, doggedly extinguished every spark that flew across the street. At another part of the fire perimeter the historic Mission Dolores, founded in 1776 and by far the oldest building in San Francisco, stood unharmed although the flames consumed every structure on the opposite side of wide Dolores Street. Even in the heart of the burned area a small number of scattered blocks and buildings remained intact. In addition to the little groups of salvaged dwellings on the summits of Russian and Telegraph hills, a section of the eastern

1906

slope of Telegraph Hill was untouched, as well as a few structures on Montgomery Street near Washington, including the old Montgomery Block, a four-story office building erected in 1853, which was saved by thick brick walls and iron shutters. Three of the exceptionally well constructed buildings belonging to the federal government withstood the fire: the brick Appraisers' Building on Sansome Street, which contained the Custom House; the Mint at Fifth and Mission streets; and the main Post Office at Seventh and Mission. Employees of the Custom House, frugally drawing water from a five-thousand-gallon tank on the roof, sprayed the falling embers and soaked the exposed wooden window frames for hours until the conflagration had swept away from the district. The Mint, built of stone and equipped on the ground floor with iron shutters, had its own artesian well, but the earthquake had damaged the pumping machinery. While this was being repaired the loyal employees used wet mops to keep the sparks from igniting the tarred roof, having first dragged a number of inflammable wooden sheds to the edge and thrown them into the courtyard. The building, containing about two hundred million dollars in bullion, was saved after seven hours of vigilance and hard work. The granite Post Office, occupying an entire block and flanked only by small wooden structures, was in a less vulnerable position, though one corner did catch fire; before the flames could spread they were extinguished by the clerks.

In the heart of the financial district, one office building survived the fire with two-thirds of its interior intact. This was the Kohl Building, an eleven-story stone-faced structure on the northeast corner of California and Montgomery streets. It was exceptionally well constructed, with the elevator shafts isolated so that they did not serve as chimneys to intensify the fire, and with all woodwork sheathed in metal. It

Opposite: The Kohl Building on the corner of California and Montgomery streets, with its four lower floors gutted by fire and seven upper floors undamaged.

also had an intelligent and efficient staff. As reported later to owner Fred Kohl, the engineer and the janitor climbed up to the roof and, filling buckets with water drawn from a tank on top of the building, extinguished the burning embers that fell onto the roof. Meanwhile sparks from an adjacent structure had started a fire in the lower floors, which the engineer and his assistant were able to check before it spread beyond control. It is probable that their efforts were aided by some quirk of air currents that steered the flames away from the building. Whatever the cause or causes may have been, the four lower floors were gutted but the seven upper stories suffered no damage at all. The Kohl Building was the only structure in the area which contained usable office space immediately after the fire.

The *Chronicle* listed a few other small islands of safety in the financial district. "One of these is the basement of the Mercantile Trust Company, on California Street, opposite the Merchants' Exchange, where even the stationery is unscorched and the furniture looks as good as it did before the fire. The basement of the Union Trust Company [at the northeast corner of Market and Montgomery streets] is in nearly as good condition"[7] These tiny oases were exceptional. Most of the large office buildings, including the Call, Chronicle, Shreve, Mills, Crocker, and Flood buildings, and the Merchants' Exchange, suffered little damage externally, but their interiors were all completely gutted. The gaunt blackened shells of these tall structures, with those of the St. Francis and Fairmont hotels and the wrecked City Hall, stood like battered monuments in the midst of miles of surrounding desolation.

Considering the magnitude of the disaster, the number of people killed or injured was remarkably small. The figures varied slightly in different accounts, but all agreed that the city's death list totaled about five hundred. Probably the most reliable estimate was that given by Maj. Gen. Adolphus

1906

Washington Greely, commander of the Division of the Pacific, in his official report dated July 30, 1906. According to this computation, 498 people were killed (including those who died later of injuries received at the time of the catastrophe) and 415 were seriously hurt but recovered. Among the dead, 194 bodies, most of them charred beyond recognition, were never identified. On the first day many corpses were hastily buried in shallow trenches dug in Portsmouth Square before any serious attempt at identification could be made; and by the time they were disinterred, several days later, and transferred to cemeteries for permanent burial, it was too late. Nearly all of the deaths were caused, directly or indirectly, by the first earthquake shock; the victims were either killed instantly by falling walls and chimneys or pinned so firmly under heaps of debris that they could not be extricated before the fire reached them. Hundreds of others, injured and half buried in rubble, were saved by heroic rescuers who, often at the risk of their own lives, dug and hacked their way through the ruins and dragged out the helpless survivors.

One reason for the relatively short death roll was the resilience of the wood-framed houses in which most San Franciscans lived. Another was the early hour; at five in the morning few people were outdoors, and as much more debris toppled into the streets than into the dwellings, the inhabitants were safer at home than anywhere else. San Francisco's 500 fatalities, in addition to approximately 250 in other communities in the earthquake zone, amounted to a small fraction of the toll which has been taken by other great earthquakes: more than 80,000 killed at Messina in 1908, for example, and at least 145,000 at Tokyo, where fire accounted for more deaths than the earthquake, in 1923.

The Metropolitan Opera Company of New York began its season of sixteen performances at the Grand Opera House in San Francisco on Monday, April 16, 1906. The opera chosen

1906

for the opening night was Karl Goldmark's *The Queen of Sheba,* conducted by Alfred Hertz and sung by Edyth Walker, Marie Rappold, Bella Alten, Andreas Dippel, Anton Van Rooy, Robert Blass, and Adolph Mühlmann. It was not an auspicious beginning. The audience that filled the large house listened politely but without enthusiasm to the undistinguished music and the mediocre voices. "Wrong opera and wrong singers," sourly commented Ashton Stevens, music critic of the *Examiner;* and the newspapers devoted more space to detailed descriptions of the elaborate gowns and jewels worn by the ladies in the boxes and orchestra seats than to the indifferent performance. Tuesday night's *Carmen* was much more successful, chiefly because of Caruso's magnificent singing in the part of Don José, though the *Examiner* criticized Olive Fremstad's interpretation of the title role as "inclined to be Dutchy" and considered Bessie Abott's Micaela "a pronounced disappointment." On Wednesday two operas were scheduled: *The Marriage of Figaro* in the afternoon, with Emma Eames, Marcella Sembrich, and Antonio Scotti in the principal roles; and *Lohengrin,* starring Marie Rappold, Louise Homer, Alois Burgstaller, and Otto Goritz, in the evening. But neither of these performances nor any of those announced for later production ever took place. By the time the curtain for the matinee was to have risen, the earthquake had rocked San Francisco, the Grand Opera House was ablaze, and the flames had already eaten their way through a large section of the city.

None of the singers and musicians of the Metropolitan Opera Company were killed or injured, but most of them lost all their personal property and, during the first day, had some exciting experiences which their artistic temperaments made the most of after they had returned safely to New York. In the Grand Opera House the flames destroyed five carloads of the Metropolitan's scenery, costumes, properties, and musical instruments, valued at $250,000 but insured for only $50,000.

The Grand Opera House on Mission Street.

Marcella Sembrich, who was at the St. Francis Hotel, lost personal effects worth about $20,000 but saved her famous pearls. Andreas Dippel and Pol Plancon also had rooms at the St. Francis. At the Palace were Caruso, Scotti, Edyth Walker, Bessie Abott, Louise Homer, Josephine Jacoby, and several other principal singers. One of the few who salvaged all his property was Caruso; with the assistance of his two valets and of Scotti, he packed three trunks, hired a garbage wagon, and drove with his luggage to the house of a friend well outside the burned area. Louise Homer fled from the hotel in a pair of her husband's trousers. Emma Eames, a guest in the house of Dr. Harry Tevis on Taylor Street near the top of Nob Hill, hurried in a borrowed car to the St. Francis and brought Sembrich to the Tevis residence, where they spent the day watching the approaching fire. That evening, as the flames began to climb the hill, Dr. Tevis, who had engaged a carriage and kept it waiting in front of the door, escorted the two singers, their maids, and his own family to North Beach, where they spent the night lying on the ground, wrapped in blankets. The next morning they made their way to the Ferry

1906

Building and crossed the bay to Oakland. Olive Fremstad, who was at the St. Dunstan, an apartment hotel on Van Ness Avenue, had a narrow escape when part of the building was damaged by the earthquake. While her maid packed her trunks (which, like Caruso, she was able to save), Fremstad worked in one of the hospitals; according to the New York *Tribune* she spent several hours "bandaging wounds and cheering the injured, carrying water and doing other menial work."[8] Later in the day the manager of her hotel found a carriage to transport the singer, her maid, and her luggage to the Ferry Building, whence they crossed to Oakland. Most of the members of the chorus and orchestra were quartered at The Oaks, a cheaper hotel on Fifth Street near the Grand Opera House. They were obliged to depart hastily, some in very scanty attire, and sought refuge in the public parks or in the houses of friends. One of the musicians was seen standing on the sidewalk in front of the hotel, clad in his underwear and clutching a violin. Alfred Hertz, one of the conductors, slept on Wednesday night at The Chutes, an amusement park—a sort of miniature Coney Island—near Golden Gate Park in the western part of the city, at which one of the entertainment features was a zoo. "To my dying day," he said afterwards, "I will never forget my experience when I was awakened by the roaring of lions. I knew not but that I was in a jungle or den of wild beasts."[9]

The first members of the opera company to arrive in New York were Fremstad and Jacoby. Fremstad had boarded an eastbound local train at Oakland on Wednesday night and caught up with the Overland Limited at Ogden on Friday morning. On the Limited she found Josephine Jacoby, and together they reached New York on the following Monday, April 23. Caruso, Sembrich, Dippel, Hertz, and several others left Oakland Friday morning on the Overland; the majority of the singers and musicians traveled east by the company's special train via New Orleans. Emma

1906

~~

Eames, who had temporarily lost her voice from exposure to the night air at North Beach, recuperated for a week at Dr. Tevis's ranch at Alma in Santa Clara County before returning to New York. The opera management, which had sold about ninety thousand dollars' worth of tickets in advance for the sixteen scheduled performances (only two of which were actually presented) at first tentatively suggested that the receipts for the uncompleted season should be donated to the relief fund for the city's refugees; but it was finally decided to return the surplus to the subscribers. For this purpose the company opened an office in San Francisco on May 17 and redeemed all tickets presented within the next thirty days.

For more than forty-eight hours after the earthquake the city was almost completely cut off from direct communication with the rest of the world. No telephones could be operated, because of damage to wires and cables. The loyal employees of the telegraph companies stuck to their posts until driven away by the flames, but there was little they could do. One wire of the Postal Telegraph Company worked intermittently during Wednesday morning. From 2:30 that afternoon until 8:30 Thursday morning all telegraphic communication ceased. Then a connection was re-established over a wire of the Southern Pacific Railroad at the Ferry Building, and for another day and night that single line provided the only telegraph service into or out of the city. By noon on Friday, Western Union, with the aid of emergency equipment furnished by the Army Signal Corps, was able to reopen an office in San Francisco and handle a limited number of messages. A day later Postal Telegraph resumed operations on a small scale, and on April 23 the cable system serving the Hawaiian Islands and the Orient was partially restored.

Telegrams describing the disaster were sent from Oakland, but the first accounts were so inaccurate and exag-

1906

gerated that the most fantastic rumors soon spread throughout the world. Newspapers in cities on the Atlantic seaboard and in Europe published vivid descriptions of an immense tidal wave which, immediately following the earthquake, had submerged and utterly destroyed the whole of San Francisco. Other journals filled their columns with gruesome reports of devastating epidemics, of the grim menace of famine, and of thousands of unburied corpses littering the streets.

The traffic in rumors traveled in both directions, usually with heavy emphasis on imaginary inundations. The inhabitants of San Francisco were told—and for a short time believed—that all of the great cities on the Atlantic coast, including New York, had been swallowed by the ocean; that Lake Michigan had risen and engulfed Chicago; that San Diego had vanished into the waters of its beautiful harbor. Nearer home, it was announced that the Cliff House, the famous San Francisco restaurant perched on a promontory overlooking the ocean, had been thrown into the water by the earthquake; and there were several "eyewitnesses" who reported that they had seen the great wooden building floating on the Pacific swells and drifting out to sea, presumably headed for Japan. Actually the Cliff House had clung sturdily to its rock, quite unharmed except for the loss of a chimney or two.

Some of the exaggerations persisted long after the true facts had been established. Months later a book compiled by an eastern publisher contained, among many other sensational and deceptive illustrations, a picture of the Chronicle and Crocker buildings toppling in blazing fragments into Market Street.[10] Their collapse was altogether fictitious; both structures survived the earthquake without a scratch, and although their interiors were gutted by the flames, they were repaired and reoccupied within a few months. Both were still standing and rendering excellent service fifty years later.

The flood of alarming rumors combined with the total

1906

~~~

lack of authentic news terrified the San Franciscans and the families and friends of San Franciscans who were living or traveling in the eastern states, in Europe, or in other parts of the globe. They dispatched thousands of telegrams and cables anxiously demanding information concerning the fate of kinfolk and friends, but the messages could not be delivered immediately, nor could the people in San Francisco send reassuring telegrams in return. Even after the telegraph offices reopened, the scanty facilities forced the companies to restrict their operations to official and press dispatches and, for several days, to refuse all individual and personal communications. Not until May 1, almost two weeks after the earthquake, was Western Union able to announce that the huge pile of accumulated messages had been transmitted and that its temporary plant at West Oakland was prepared to handle future business at normal speed. Mail service into and out of the city was also very irregular and subject to delay for some time; almost half the people had been burned out and thousands had left the city, so that it was impossible to locate some of the addressees.

Every newspaper plant in San Francisco was destroyed on the first day or during the first night of the fire. Nevertheless the reporters continued to work like beavers, inspecting the damage caused by the earthquake, listening to accounts of heroic rescues and hairbreadth escapes, retreating before the flames as they spread from building to building and from street to street, scribbling notes about everything they saw and heard, and even attempting, only a few hours after the earthquake, to estimate the number of casualties and the amount of property loss. As soon as it became obvious that none of the city presses would survive, the managing editors of the three morning dailies held a conference and decided to publish a joint edition of their papers. That night the Oakland *Tribune* hospitably placed its plant and press at their disposal, and on Thursday morning several thousand copies

1906

of a four-page newspaper headed *The Call-Chronicle-Examiner* were distributed gratuitously to San Francisco newsboys, who reaped a harvest of small change.

The production of this little paper under such conditions was one of the most remarkable feats in the history of journalism. The entire issue was devoted to one subject: the disaster that had overtaken San Francisco. There were no advertisements and no pictures. Most of the front page, printed in large capitals, gave a condensed account of the earthquake, the progress of the conflagration, and the ineffectual attempts to check the flames. Considering the confusion in the city on that first day, the rumors, the exaggerations, the conflicting reports, and the advancing walls of flame that kept the newsmen from penetrating into many areas, the information was astonishingly accurate—much more accurate than most of the newspaper accounts published on the same morning in other California cities. There were, perhaps inevitably, a few purple passages as well as a few unduly pessimistic forecasts. "Death and Destruction have been the fate of San Francisco," announced the first line of the front page. And lower down: "Everybody in San Francisco is prepared to leave the city, for the belief is firm that San Francisco will be totally destroyed. . . . Men worked like fiends to combat the laughing, roaring, onrushing fire demons." But on the whole the tone of the paper was sober and factual. To the people of the isolated city, most of whom knew little about what had happened outside of their own neighborhoods, it brought the first comprehensive account of the disaster. Today the surviving copies of the thin triple-headed newspaper dated April 19, 1906 are treasured as rare collectors' items, and reprinted facsimiles are still in demand.

A few hours after the earthquake Mayor Eugene Schmitz summoned a number of prominent citizens to a meeting, which assembled early on Wednesday afternoon in the base-

1906

～

ment of the Hall of Justice on Kearny Street. The group, usually called the Committee of Fifty although the number was in fact somewhat larger, comprised representatives of many professions and businesses: lawyers, doctors, clergymen of various denominations, architects, bankers, wholesale and retail merchants, industrialists, public utility officials, real estate dealers, newspaper owners. During the first session the fire came so close to the building that the committee moved hastily across the street to Portsmouth Square; but the intense heat soon made the little park untenable, and the conference retreated up Nob Hill to the unfinished Fairmont Hotel, where it remained for the rest of the day. When the committee attempted to return to the Fairmont on Thursday morning the flames were already sweeping through the great empty structure, so the next meeting took place at the North End police station. Within a few hours the harassed citizens again found themselves in the path of the fire, and at noon on Thursday they established their fifth, and final, headquarters in Franklin Hall on Fillmore Street near Sutter, well beyond the western limit of the conflagration. There the members of the committee, at last able to work without interruption, prepared to deal with the urgent and complex problems created by the emergency.

The first step was the organization of twenty subcommittees, with the most importance being assigned to Relief of the Hungry, Housing of the Homeless, Relief of Sick and Wounded, Transportation of Refugees, Citizens' Police, Restoration of Water Supply, Finance, Sanitation, and—for the benefit of posterity—History and Statistics. During the first few days the municipal government practically abdicated and turned over its functions to the various subcommittees, though the mayor served as general chairman of the Committee of Fifty and signed the orders and decrees proposed by its members. The first, and one of the most important, of these was a proclamation issued over the mayor's signature on the

Looters on Sutter Street.

first day of the fire: "The federal troops, the members of the regular police force, and all special police officers have been authorized to KILL any and all persons found engaged in looting or the commission of any other crimes." The proclamation, of which five thousand copies, hurriedly printed on a handpress, were immediately distributed throughout the city, further directed that "the gas and electric lighting companies must not turn on gas nor electricity until I order them to do so," and also that "all citizens remain at home from darkness until daylight of every night until order is restored." The irony of this last injunction did not fail to strike the citizens, half of whom no longer had any homes to remain in. The edict authorizing the killing of looters and other felons, though it probably did help to reduce the number of crimes, was altogether illegal. At no time was martial law in effect, in spite of a general impression that it was—an impression fostered by an erroneous announcement in the combined *Call-Chronicle-Examiner* of April 19 that "under a special message from President [Theodore] Roosevelt, the city was placed under martial law." The military forces contributed

1906

invaluable assistance to the relief of the city, but their commanders were scrupulously careful at all times to cooperate with, not to supersede, the civilian authorities.

From the very beginning the army played a vital part in fighting the fire, maintaining order, feeding the destitute, providing shelter for the homeless, and caring for the sick and injured. On April 16 the commanding officer, Major General Greely, had departed for the east on leave. News of the disaster reached him as his train was passing through Omaha. He proceeded to Chicago, then returned immediately to San Francisco, arriving on the fourth day after the earthquake. During his absence Brig. Gen. Frederick Funston temporarily assumed command of the Division of the Pacific. Very early on Wednesday morning General Funston, observing the rapid spread of the conflagration and realizing that the municipal police could not possibly cope with the situation without assistance, dispatched urgent messages to the three military posts in the city—the Presidio, Fort Mason, and Fort Miley—to send troops to his headquarters in the Phelan Building on Market Street. Before eight o'clock two companies from the nearest post, Fort Mason, were guarding the financial district and patrolling Market Street to prevent looting. A few minutes later a larger detachment from the Presidio arrived. Some of the men were ordered to guard the Mint and Post Office; the rest were assigned to additional street patrols. The troops from Fort Miley, in the northwest corner of the city near the Cliff House, were obliged to march five miles and reached the Phelan Building shortly before noon, when they too were put to work. By that time thousands of people had filtered into the downtown area, some in the hope of salvaging property and records from their shops and offices, others merely to watch the progress of the fire and the futile efforts of the firemen to arrest it. The soldiers drove back the crowds and established a cordon around the danger zones, permitting nobody to go through except officials and

Refugee tents at Fort Mason.

reporters provided with improvised passes. Afterwards these rigid military rules, strictly enforced by the troops, became the targets of severe criticism on the ground that a great deal of portable property, especially documents, might have been rescued if the owners had been allowed access to their premises. This was probably true, but such precautions and restrictions, even if excessive in some instances, saved a good many lives.

Some of the soldiers (including General Funston) remained on duty for more than forty-eight hours without relief, but it soon became evident that the number of troops stationed in the city could not handle all the work that had to be done, even with the assistance of detachments from Alcatraz and Angel Island in the bay and from Fort Baker in Marin County across the Golden Gate. There was a large garrison at Monterey, one hundred miles south of San Francisco, but the telegraph lines in that direction, even from Oakland, had ceased to function. At General Funston's request, Admiral Goodrich of the Pacific Squadron sent a fast torpedo boat to

Refugee houses at the Presidio.

Monterey with orders for reinforcements, and two days later several battalions arrived. Funston also ordered the commanding officer at Vancouver Barracks on the Columbia River to proceed southward by train with his entire garrison, which reached San Francisco on April 22 and 23. Within a week after the earthquake about six thousand soldiers of the regular army were on duty in the city. In addition, the navy contributed more than one thousand officers and sailors and a force of naval apprentices from Mare Island to patrol the waterfront; a detachment of marines took charge of another area; and Governor Pardee sent a brigade of the militia, the National Guard of California, to San Francisco and smaller detachments to Santa Rosa, San Jose, and Oakland. Rumors of grave dissension between the army and the civil authorities appear to have been unfounded—in any event they were promptly and vigorously denied by both Mayor Schmitz and General Greely—but clashes between the militia and the civilians were not infrequent.

1906

Endless streams of men, women, and children, driven from their homes by the fire, trudged wearily up the hills to the parks and open spaces of the Western Addition all day Wednesday, all Wednesday night, and again from dawn to dark on Thursday. The more level-headed refugees carried suitcases or sacks filled with useful articles: canned food, blankets, serviceable clothing, a few pots and pans. Not a few went empty-handed; others burdened themselves with possessions which, whatever their intrinsic or sentimental value may have been, were worthless in an emergency: heavy silverware, china tea-sets, elaborate evening dresses and feathered hats, empty birdcages, oil paintings, clocks, "hand- painted" ornaments. Some, puffing and panting, pushed pianos up the steep hills, more or less wrecking the instruments en route. Many people dragged heavy furniture and hastily packed trunks out of their houses, only to abandon them on the sidewalks for lack of transportation. No streetcars were running; the few automobiles in the city were still rich men's toys in 1906; there were not nearly enough horse-drawn vehicles to convey the household gear of two hundred thousand suddenly displaced persons, and many of the wagons had been commandeered by the Committee of Fifty for the transportation of food and hospital supplies, while the drivers of most of the remaining conveyances demanded exorbitant prices. The refugees put to use everything they owned that would roll or slide, everything that could be pushed or pulled: handcarts, wheelbarrows, toy brakewagons, baby carriages, even sewing machines were piled high with salvaged possessions and hauled over the cobbles.

The lucky fugitives with friends or relatives in the Western Addition or in the remoter districts of the Mission

Refugees standing in line for the distribution of clothing and household gear.

had no trouble in finding shelter and hospitality, but they were in the minority. By Wednesday evening homeless families filled all of the small parks west of Van Ness Avenue—Jefferson Square, Lafayette Square, Alta Plaza, Hamilton Square, Alamo Square, Buena Vista Park, and others—and overflowed into the larger and more distant open spaces of Golden Gate Park and the Presidio. Some camped out in vacant lots; some took up improvised lodgings in the stalled cable-cars. Those who had brought rugs or blankets spread them on the ground; the others simply stood or sat or stretched out on the grass. There was no privacy for anyone; neither, at first, were there any toilet facilities. The smaller squares were uncomfortably crowded, but in general a friendly, all-in-the-same-boat spirit prevailed. Families stayed together as much as possible and tried hard not to spill over onto the plots occcupied by adjoining groups a few inches away. Even the children were generally quiet and well behaved, though some of the youngsters, welcoming the abrupt break

A typical block of outdoor kitchens.

in routine as an exciting adventure, chased each other over the congested lawns, played leapfrog over their recumbent neighbors, and got in everybody's way. There was not much for anyone to do that first day except to watch the dense clouds of smoke that darkened the sky and to guess which areas would be the next to burn. That night the people clustering on the western hilltops stared in awe at the bright red glow reflected from the smoke and at the immense wall of orange flame, subsiding in a shower of sparks at one spot, flaring up at another, and always creeping nearer as the slow hours passed. The spectacle was horrifying, but it was also magnificent and, in a curious way, beautiful. At times the onlookers could almost forget that a great city—their own city— was being destroyed before their eyes, and imagine that they were witnessing an Olympian display of fireworks provided by the gods for their entertainment.

Yet many of the refugees, worn out by excitement, the early awakening, and the long walk to safety, slept soundly in the open air that night, with or without blankets. The weather was mild, neither hot nor cold, though the heat from the

1906

~~

fire raised the temperature a few degrees above normal. Those who had brought food ate a little and shared what they had with less provident neighbors; but on that first day nobody except the children thought very much about eating. The scarcity of drinking water presented a much more serious problem. Here and there a few hydrants, fed by some local reservoirs through pipe that happened to remain intact, continued to function, but these rare sources were too scanty and too scattered to be of much use. To relieve the immediate shortage on Wednesday, Admiral McCalla sent fifty thousand gallons of fresh water by barge from Mare Island, and more came by boat from Oakland and Goat Island. The Board of Public Works filled its carts, normally used for sprinkling the streets, with this precious water and distributed it sparingly, not only to the refugees but also to the other thirsty inhabitants; for even those whose dwellings were undamaged had no water.

Although there had been no anti-Oriental demonstrations in San Francisco for many years, the Chinese had always lived in their own quarter and had had little social contact with the rest of the population. Racial prejudice still existed, and not even catastrophe could eradicate it. To avoid "incidents" the Committee of Fifty decided to establish the Chinese and Japanese refugees in a separate camp covering four square blocks at the northern end of Franklin Street near Fort Mason, where the army had provided tents and latrines for them; but when certain white citizens objected that it might be difficult to dislodge the Orientals from the site later on, the camp was moved to the Presidio on April 27. It was one of the most peaceful and orderly camps in the city, but it was not popular; most of the Asians left San Francisco as soon as they could, and by the end of July only fifty occupants remained. Another Chinese camp, located in Oakland, was considered by General Greely "probably the best camp in the city."[11] Neither the Japanese nor Chinese refugees asked for

1906

~~~

much assistance from the general relief organization; well aware of the antipathy felt towards them by a small but articulate and aggressive minority of white San Franciscans, they preferred to depend on their own people. A Japanese Relief Association, organized two days after the earthquake and financed by Japanese throughout California, sent between seven thousand and eight thousand of their fellow countrymen out of the city and contributed to their support until they could find work in other communities. Chinese organizations made similar arrangements for the care of their own refugees.

While the homeless multitudes were tramping along the streets leading to the west, almost as many people were moving in the opposite direction, eastward by circuitous routes skirting the burning areas to the Ferry Building at the foot of Market Street. Within two hours after the earthquake the ferryboats were running on practically normal schedules to Oakland and Alameda on the east side of the bay and to Tiburon and Sausalito on the north. By noon many suburban trains across the bay had started to operate in spite of damage caused by the earthquake: broken switches, overturned water tanks, and the cessation of telephonic and telegraphic communication between stations.

The great majority of those who left the city traveled no more than ten or fifteen miles. They settled down in temporary quarters in Oakland, Berkeley (where parts of the University of California campus were thrown open for their reception), Alameda, Fruitvale, San Leandro, and dozens of other communities on the eastern side of the bay, as well as in San Rafael and other nearby towns in Marin County. A few had country houses of their own, some found accommodation with friends or relatives, but most were herded into refugee camps improvised by local relief committees. The peak of the exodus was reached on Thursday, when the Southern Pacific transported more than one thousand cars full of refugees.

72

1906

During the first eight days after the earthquake the Southern Pacific alone carried more than 300,000 passengers by ferry and train out of San Francisco: 226,000 to suburban towns across the bay, 67,000 to more distant points in California, and about 7,700 to other states. The figures for suburban travel are somewhat misleading, as a good many people shuttled back and forth during that period and were counted several times, but it is certain that at least 225,000—about half the population—moved out of the city for several weeks or months. All of these passengers were transported free of charge, at an estimated cost to the railroad company of $456,000. Although for years the Southern Pacific had been execrated throughout California for its ruthlessness, its grasping and often illegal acquisition of vast tracts of public land, and its corruption of the state legislature and other officials, the company's generosity and efficiency during the emergency wiped out much of the accumulated resentment.

The Santa Fe Railroad, with its single line terminating at Richmond on the east side of the bay, suffered considerable damage from the earthquake, but by six o'clock on Wednesday afternoon, as soon as gangs of workmen had completed temporary repairs to rails and switches, this company also placed all of its facilities at the disposal of the refugees without charge, and transported additional thousands to destinations along its route. For the first three or four days the only people who escaped from San Francisco by land to the suburbs located on the peninsula to the south were those who owned or were able to hire automobiles or carriages, for the Southern Pacific tracks in that direction were torn up by the earthquake, and in one place a few miles outside of the city limits the roadbed had sunk twenty feet. Nevertheless the company's engineers, working night and day, managed to repair the line sufficiently to permit six trains to run to San Jose on Saturday, April 21, and ten on Sunday. Within another week local service between San Francisco and San Jose was

1906

almost normal, but for about a month, until street cars were again in operation to the terminus at Third and Townsend Streets, all Southern Pacific through-trains to and from Los Angeles were routed via the San Joaquin Valley to Oakland.

Eight days after the earthquake the railroads discontinued the indiscriminate free transportation of passengers. The Committee of Fifty then opened a transportation bureau on Fillmore Street, in charge of a secretary who personally interviewed all applicants for free travel. Petitioners who could prove that they were actually destitute received passes, and those who had some money but not enough for the full fare were required to pay part (never more than half) of the price. After May 10 no more free or reduced-rate tickets were issued.

By no means all of the people who fled from San Francisco were homeless refugees. Many well-to-do families whose houses remained intact sent their women and children, and the elderly members of their households, to the suburbs or the country, to rented houses or resort hotels, to friends or relatives in other cities. Such flights were not inspired by panic, for there was practically no panic at any time; but at first it did seem at least possible that the earthquake and fire might be followed by famine or epidemic, or both. Even if the city escaped these horrors—as in fact it did—it would certainly be an uncomfortable place to live in for some time. From a practical standpoint the departure of thousands of the weaker, less immediately useful inhabitants was of great benefit to those who were left: it meant fewer mouths to feed, less work for the overburdened relief committees, more time to be devoted to the urgent problems of rehabilitation. Most of the able-bodied men of these families stayed in the city, camping out in their waterless, lightless houses, to salvage what they could of their businesses or professions and to make plans for the future.

1906

"Famine and Death, twin children of Fire, stalked in the wake of their father today," announced an edition of the San Francisco *Examiner* printed on the presses of the Los Angeles *Examiner* two days after the earthquake. "San Francisco is being starved to death. . . . What little supply of bread there is, is being sold for a dollar a loaf." The situation was not nearly as grim as the journal's florid prose led its readers to believe, but it was nevertheless fortunate that few of the adults in San Francisco felt very hungry on the first day of the fire. The great storage warehouses containing the bulk of the food supply burned early that day. Within a few hours most of the retail provision stores—bakeries, corner groceries, butcher shops, delicatessens—in the undestroyed residence districts were cleaned out by provident purchasers. In spite of the apocryphal dollar-a-loaf story from Los Angeles, almost none of these establishments raised their prices; nor did more than a few buyers attempt to hoard more than they needed for a day or two. By far the greater number of refugees in the parks and squares had no food at all, and by Thursday they were extremely hungry.

The efficient commissary department of the army, which swung promptly into action under General Funston's orders, averted the immediate threat of famine. Although the principal military storehouses containing supplies worth two million dollars were destroyed by fire on Wednesday, the bakeries at the Presidio worked overtime. On Thursday the soldiers distributed vast quantitites of bread, hot coffee, canned corned beef, milk and other provisions, without charge. The War Department also shipped nine hundred thousand army rations from the posts at Vancouver Barracks, Seattle, and Los Angeles. Meanwhile the troops and the police had broken into about one hundred small food shops which were in the path of the fire or, for one reason or another, had remained closed, confiscated the contents after making sketchy inventories for the purpose of future compensation, and doled out the provisions to the refugees.

By Friday the Committee of Fifty's Subcommittee for Relief of the Hungry began to function. Its first act was to arrange for the immediate inspection of the chimneys of such bakeries as had survived, and for the baking of bread in those that were undamaged. That day the bakeries furnished thirty-five thousand loaves, and the supply of bread increased rapidly thereafter. The chairman of the subcommittee reported, perhaps a little too optimistically, that on Friday night "not a hungry soul existed in San Francisco."[12]

Almost as important as the distribution of food was the provision of emergency shelter and clothing for the refugees. In these departments the army again took the lead. During the first three days the quartermaster at the Presidio issued three thousand tents, thirteen thousand ponchos, fifty-eight thousand shoes, and twenty-four thousand shirts, as well as blankets and other articles. Unable to communicate with Washington by telegraph, and in the absence of his superior General Greely, Funston was obliged to order the distribution of this government property, including the commissary food, and to mobilize his troops for patrol and fire-fighting duty, entirely on his own responsibility. After telegraph service was restored he sent a report to the Secretary of War, William Howard Taft, explaining the situation and adding that he expected all of his actions to be approved. They were.

As soon as the first news of the disaster spread throughout the world, relief supplies of all kinds began to pour into San Francisco. Practically every community in California and every city in the United States promptly sent generous contri-

1906

butions of food, tents, bedding, household equipment, and medical supplies.

Because of the relatively short distances they had to travel, the first shipments to reach the city came from the Pacific Coast states. The steamship *Roanoke,* chartered by the Los Angeles *Examiner* and speedily loaded with hundreds of tons of provisions, started northward only about forty hours after the earthquake. The first trainload from Chicago arrived in Oakland on April 22. During the first four weeks more than thirteen hundred carloads of miscellaneous supplies aggregating 26,000 tons came to the city by rail, in addition to 5,700 tons carried by steamer. The Southern Pacific, Santa Fe, and other railroads transported all of these contributions free of charge; the cost to Southern Pacific alone, the principal carrier, amounted to almost five hundred thousand dollars, in addition to the approximately equal sum expended by the company for free passenger travel. All along the routes from the east the passenger trains, including the crack Overland Limited, were unceremoniously shunted onto sidings while the long strings of freight cars sped by on their way to the Oakland terminus. Edward H. Harriman, president of the Southern Pacific, announced: "I have issued orders that the situation in San Francisco is to be considered above everything else;" and to make sure that his orders would be effectively carried out he hastened from New York to San Francisco in his special train. Throughout the summer the relief shipments continued, though in diminishing quantities as the need decreased. By the end of November, 1,850 carloads of donated provisions and 150 carloads of clothing had arrived in the city.

Liberal gifts of money also flowed into San Francico. Congress appropriated two and a half million dollars, though only about three hundred thousand dollars reached the relief committee in cash; the government expended the balance for food and other articles. A number of benefit performances,

1906

special concerts, raffles, and similar entertainments were organized in various places to raise money for the San Francisco refugees. Sarah Bernhardt, then on an American tour, presented a play from her repertoire in a huge tent in Chicago and donated the proceeds to the fund. In New York a monster production of musical, dramatic, and vaudeville numbers, sponsored by the associated theater managers, took place at the Metropolitan Opera House on May 4. "The big benefit," reported the San Francisco *Chronicle,* "yielded something like $35,000, which will go to relieve the needs of theatrical people and police who suffered in the recent conflagration. The police of New York sold 14,000 tickets . . . and in addition . . . $4000 was realized from the sale of flowers, programmes and souvenirs. The performance started at 11 o'clock in the morning and . . . was not concluded until 2 o'clock the following morning. There was a general outpouring of the theatrical and musical talent. . . ." The same paper announced that "Blanche Bates, Margaret Anglin, Katherine Grey, Minnie Dupree, Maude Knowlton and Ada Lewis, gave a fair at the Belasco Theater [in New York] . . . that netted big results, and Joe Weber and Marie Dressler conducted a bazaar at the Gilsey House where contributed articles were sold, the chorus girls of the Weber company performing the duties of salesladies."[13]

Generous offers of financial assistance from other countries came through embassies and legations in Washington, but President Roosevelt refused all of these and declared that the United States could take care of its own distressed citizens. The refusals aroused a good deal of resentment among the inhabitants of San Francisco, whose wishes had not been consulted. "It goes without saying," indignantly protested the weekly *Argonaut,* "that the people of our afflicted State do not agree with the President. . . . The Empress Dowager of China has offered a personal contribution of seventy-five thousand dollars. . . . The Japanese Government has also offered . . . 100,000 yen, which has similarly been declined. The Republic of Mexico voted . . . $30,000; declined. The Republic of Guatemala offered $10,000; declined. The Government of New Zealand offered $25,000. . . . The little island of Martinique offered 10,000 francs. . . . The municipality of Edmondson [sic], Canada, offered $1000. . . . Many municipalities, corporations, and individuals in Germany, France, Cuba, and other countries have also offered aid. All of these offers have been declined."[14] Nevertheless some foreign nations or individuals residing therein did make unofficial contributions to the relief fund. A survey by the Russell Sage Foundation listed the following cash donations:

Austria	$50.00
Australia	385.96
Belgium	50.00
Canada	145,412.65
Cape Colony (Americans)	464.00
Ceylon	32.33
China	40,000.00
Cuba	734.30
England	6,570.88
France (American Chamber of Commerce, Paris, $20,850)	21,235.08
Germany	50.00
Japan	244,960.10
Mexico	14,480.31
Russia	199.02
Scotland	50.40
Colombia (Americans)	200.00

Citizens of San Francisco itself contributed $413,090.83 in cash, and about twenty-five hundred cities and towns in the United States donated $8,228,978.25, mak-

1906

ing a grand total of $9,116,944.11, not including the monies appropriated by Congress and numerous independent funds. The most touching donation came from the leper colony on the Hawaiian island of Molokai, where more than four hundred of the wretched, incurable (at that time), and practically destitute patients held a meeting, adopted "eloquently worded resolutions in the Hawaiian language expressing sympathy for the sufferers from the San Francisco fire," and raised a fund of $194.55 composed of individual offerings ranging upward from five cents apiece.[15]

When the earthquake wrecked the City Hall, the Receiving Hospital in one of the wings was so severely damaged that it was no longer serviceable. The patients (none of whom, luckily, were hurt by the quake) were carried across the street to the Mechanics' Pavilion, an immense wooden building occupying an entire square block and normally used for conventions and similar gatherings. This was quickly converted into an emergency hospital to which about three hundred additional patients, injured by toppling walls and chimneys, were brought early on Wednesday morning. Doctors and nurses volunteered their services; drugstores were broken into and their stocks of surgical and medical supplies confiscated; mattresses, pillows, sheets, and blankets were filched from doomed department stores. Surgeons performed scores of emergency operations on the wounded, who lay on rough planks supported by trestles.

The improvised hospital lasted only a few hours. By noon the flames sweeping eastward from the Hayes Valley "ham-and-egg" fire were approaching the Mechanics' Pavilion, and a horrible rumor spread through the city that all of the helpless patients had burned to death. Like most of the rumors in circulation that day, this was fortunately quite untrue. Every patient was hastily moved, in commandeered automobiles and wagons, to the Presidio, some only a few minutes before the Pavilion burst into flame.

1906

~~~

At least one hundred other injured persons were treated at the Harbor Hospital near the waterfront, where navy doctors and nurses transported by boat from Mare Island assisted the regular staff. Although the army's General Hospital had sustained some earthquake damage and was handicapped by lack of water and a disabled power plant, it continued to function and to receive injured civilians. Other army hospitals at the Presidio and Fort Mason, in addition to hurriedly erected tent hospitals, accommodated the overflow, and a few days later a military field hospital for the refugees in Golden Gate Park and a two-hundred-bed hospital for contagious diseases at Harbor View Park were established. The army's General Hospital furnished free medical supplies.

According to another sensational but baseless rumor, the fire had consumed the jails and roasted alive the prisoners in their locked cells. In fact all of the prisoners were escorted under guard to Alcatraz, Mare Island, and other places of detention, whence they were subsequently reassembled in the undamaged branch jails at Ingleside in the southwest corner of the city.

For a few days the hundreds of injured victims of the earthquake filled all of the permanent and improvised hospitals and made heavy demands on the overworked doctors and nurses. With the exception of these sufferers the people of San Francisco remained almost incredibly healthy. The dreaded epidemics so dolefully predicted in out-of-town newspapers failed to materialize. In that temperate climate the enforced outdoor life entailed no real hardships, and the restricted but wholesome diet agreed with almost all of the refugees. Babies were born in the parks—some prematurely on account of shock and excitement—without the aid of obstetricians or professional nurses, but the primitive conditions apparently did little harm to either mothers or infants. The refugees did, however, suffer acute discomfort during a heavy downpour that drenched the city on Sunday night and Monday morning, April 22 and 23. Most of the homeless were still without

1906

tents; in Golden Gate Park alone ten thousand people had no shelter but the dripping trees; many had only a single blanket or poncho apiece, and some had not even that much covering. "Hundreds . . . went without their breakfasts," reported the *Examiner,* "the food at the nearest supply stations being badly damaged by the damp, and the drenching of fuel made it practically impossible to build fires for making coffee. . . . At the Presidio the different encampments of refugees were steaming sodden collections of discomfort." But not even the rain, disagreeable as it was, had any deleterious effect on the health of the soggy campers. As soon as the storm began, Mayor Schmitz and Chief of Police Dinan sent out police details to commandeer vacant houses and flats, and eventually about two thousand people were established in such dwellings, with or without permission of the owners. Another rainstorm, the last before the onset of the dry season, occurred a month later, but by that time all of the refugees were under shelter.

Four weeks after the earthquake, although the great exodus of the first few days had drained off thousands of homeless people, about fifty thousand refugees were still living in the city in more than one hundred separate camps, of which twenty-one were under military control. In the carefully supervised military camps and in the large tent communities in Golden Gate Park sanitary conditions were satisfactory, but in many of the smaller squares the only facilities were hastily dug latrines. With no water in the mains, occupants of the houses which escaped the fire also had to improvise cesspools and build little outhouses in their back yards. Yet the lack of proper sanitation caused very little, if any, illness. Refugees and householders used disinfectants lavishly and boiled all their drinking water. In the first two months the authorities reported only ninety-five cases of typhoid, with seventeen deaths. The daily average of sick people

1906

among all the refugees amounted to less than three percent. The general health was so extraordinarily rugged that after the first week the various emergency hospitals, established to care for the injured, were no longer needed, and the medical attendants whose services had been in such demand for a few days soon found themselves with nothing to do. Hundreds of doctors and nurses who came to San Francisco from other cities to cope with the anticipated epidemics were sent home. Many of the local physicians had lost not only their offices and equipment but most of their regular patients, a great many of whom, especially the wealthier ones, had left the city. Hypochondriacs miraculously recovered from their imaginary ailments under emergency conditions. As a precautionary measure the army and civil authorities opened twenty-six dispensaries in various parts of the city, where free medical attendance and supplies were made available to every applicant; but what General Greely called "the not unreasonable complaints of destitute doctors and druggists" quickly brought about the abolition of all but one of these clinics.[16]

At first President Roosevelt, unaware that the local Committee of Fifty and its subcommittees were speedily and efficiently dealing with the various phases of relief, had proposed to place the Red Cross in control of the work; but when the special representative of the Red Cross, Dr. Edward T. Devine, arrived in San Francisco he perceived at once that no such reorganization was necessary. Instead, he cooperated enthusiastically and effectively with the committee and the army. A few weeks later, when the most urgent problems had been solved, all of the subcommittees were abolished except that on Finance, which then combined with the Red Cross under a new title: San Francisco Relief and Red Cross Funds. This organization, authorized to receive, disburse, and account for millions of dollars, was legally incorporated and was usually referred to as the Relief Corporation.

The food supplies contributed by the army and by generous donors throughout the nation were distributed from relief stations or "bread lines" scattered over the unburned sections of the city. On April 29 the number of these stations reached a maximum of 177. Applicants for food during the first week or two included practically all the inhabitants who remained in San Francisco, the wealthy as well as the destitute, those whose houses had been preserved as well as the homeless refugees, for no provisions were obtainable except from the relief stations. For several weeks the bread lines gave out an average of three hundred thousand rations a day, and although this number was drastically reduced as commercial shipments restocked the shops and people who had money or charge accounts could buy their own provisions, a total of almost eight million daily rations or twenty-four million free meals had been issued by June 30. The rations consisted of bread, fresh meat and vegetables when available, canned food, potatoes, sugar, coffee, tea, milk, and similar staples. In the parks and squares each family or group built its own little fire, made its own coffee or tea, and cooked its own food. People whose dwellings had not been destroyed were also obliged to do their cooking *al fresco,* for indoor fires were forbidden until chimneys had been inspected and, if necessary, repaired. Each householder set up a little stove on the sidewalk in front of his residence and often enclosed it in a rough wooden shed to protect it from the wind and keep the sparks from flying.

The heterogeneous shipments of food sent by hundreds of different communities naturally resulted in an oversupply of some commodities and a more or less serious shortage of others. In a few instances, especially at the beginning, the selections appeared to owe more to the good hearts than to the good sense of the donors. "Huge consignments of

1906

sandwiches that have come in from nearby points," reported the *Examiner* on April 26, "are being thrown away because they are useless in the condition in which they arrive. The wiser ones . . . have sent hard boiled eggs." Contributions of potatoes and flour were far in excess of the requirements. Tons of potatoes sprouted and rotted; flour was issued to anyone who asked for it, but there was little demand because neither the bonfires of the refugees nor the makeshift sidewalk kitchens had any facilities for baking. The Relief Corporation therefore sold its flour to the rehabilitated commercial bakeries (which could not obtain it elsewhere) and bought it back in the form of bread at a fixed price. After the corporation had received its quota the bakeries were permitted to sell the surplus bread at ten cents a loaf in quantities of not more than five loaves to one purchaser. This arrangement caused an unfortunate misunderstanding between the Relief Corporation and the local relief committee in Minneapolis, which, unfamiliar with the situation in San Francisco, resented the sale of its donations and indignantly demanded the distribution of the uncooked flour to the consumers for whom it was intended. General Greely, irritated by the controversy, suggested that the flour should be returned to Minneapolis; but explanations eventually convinced the irate donors that their flour was being used for the benefit of the refugees in the most efficient, and indeed the only possible, way.

During the first week provisions were distributed without question to everyone standing in the bread lines. Then the army and the Relief Corporation, unwilling to perpetuate habits of dependence among the refugees, decided to refuse free rations to all able-bodied men (for whom there was no lack of paid employment in removing debris and other rehabilitation projects) and to issue supplies only to women, children, the aged, the infirm, and the congenitally unemployable. The Red Cross undertook to register all of the refugees, and by May 7 cards had been printed which, when

∿

filled out by applicants properly qualified under the new rules, entitled the holders to receive rations. These cards also provided for the distribution of special foods, such as fresh meat, milk, butter, eggs, vegetables, and fruit, to those who could prove their need of them. Another use to which the cards were put was the elimination of "repeaters." Though the great majority of the refugees took no more food than they actually required, a certain number—estimated by General Greely at two percent—habitually roamed from one bread line to another and accumulated far more than they and their families were able to eat. The registration cards effectively weeded them out.

To feed the able-bodied men who were thus deprived of their rations, communal kitchens were established in various parts of the city, at which hot meals were served for fifteen cents apiece; to applicants who could not afford even that small sum the Red Cross issued free meal tickets. The first of these kitchens, operated by the Desmond Construction Company under contract, opened on May 12. By June 21 the number had increased to twenty-seven, run by three contractors. These kitchens, with their rows of long wooden tables, were temporary stopgaps designed primarily to discourage dependence on charity and to force the healthy wage-earning refugees to support themselves and their families and to buy their provisions in the undestroyed retail shops, most of which had replenished their stocks by the middle of May. This stern but wise policy quickly produced the expected result. In two months the number standing in the bread lines was reduced more than ninety-five percent, from 325,000 on April 30 to about 15,000 on June 30. Those still on relief after that date comprised the truly destitute who, for one reason or another, were unable to work.

Clothing, cots, bedding, and household equipment contributed by sympathizers all over the nation were issued from depots set up in two or three of the public schools. Dur-

1906

ing the first two weeks these articles were given to all who asked for them, but the rapacity of a few refugees who took advantage of this openhandedness to acquire extensive wardrobes soon put an end to the unregulated system. On May 4 the army took charge of the reception, sorting, and distribution, and the Red Cross determined which applicants were entitled to supplies and which were merely trying to get something for nothing. General Greely estimated that about two hundred thousand people received one or more articles of clothing before the end of July, when the distribution practically ceased. It must be admitted that by no means all of the wearing apparel reflected great credit upon the taste and generosity of the donors. Many of the contributions "bore the well-known mark of the charity gift."[17] Some of the new garments came from unsalable stocks, of poor quality and in odd unusable sizes; much of the old clothing, dragged out of trunks and attics, had to be cleaned and disinfected, and some was so dirty and ragged that it had to be thrown away. Not a few of the women's dresses and hats were so grotesquely old-fashioned that they could have served as costumes for a Civil War melodrama; not even the destitute would accept them.

1906

The abrupt displacement of hundreds of thousands of people, scattered in more than one hundred refugee camps within the city as well as in all the suburbs and in more distant communities, made it extremely difficult for members of families to locate each other or even to discover promptly whether they were dead or alive, sick or well, injured or unharmed. Friends could not find other friends; businessmen were unable to get in touch with their employees. In their efforts to exchange information the homeless resorted to some curious makeshifts, such as tacking hundreds of scribbled names and addresses to a fence near Golden Gate Park. Two days after the earthquake the Committee of Fifty opened a registration office at which the people remaining in San Francisco could file their temporary addresses and look up those of other refugees. But the most effective service was rendered by the newspapers, all of which, immediately after the issue of the combined *Call-Chronicle-Examiner* on April 19, borrowed the facilities of Oakland journals and resumed independent publication. For several weeks the papers carried long lists in fine print—sometimes as many as twelve columns in a single issue—of new addresses as well as anxious inquiries concerning the welfare and locations of families and friends. Among the hundreds of personal communications in the *Examiner* of April 21, the following are typical:

"A. B. Seal wants his mother, Sarah Seal, to come to 607 Third Avenue. He would like knowledge of her whereabouts."

"Madame Tully will find her husband camped in a Sutter-street car opposite 1902 Sutter street."

"Dr. Charles V. Cross is rendering free service to the needy in the vicinity of California and Divisadero streets."

1906

Addresses filed at the registration bureau and printed in the newspapers enabled the Post Office to function after a fashion three days after the earthquake. A day later the first mails destined for other cities left San Francisco, some of the letters being written on scraps of paper, shingles, soiled cuffs, and other unorthodox substitutes for stationery. The postmen struggled valiantly against immense difficulties to deliver mail to those whose addresses were known. Although the main post office had survived both earthquake and fire, the streets surrounding it were torn up, choked with debris, and almost impassable. Many of the branch offices were destroyed. At one time fifteen hundred tons of undelivered second class mail piled up at the Oakland terminus.

Within a few days new business addresses began to appear in the papers in the form of small advertisements. Wholesale and retail merchants, brokers, steamship agents, real estate dealers, doctors, attorneys, and other business and professional people established temporary offices in their own houses (if these had escaped destruction), in rented houses in the Western Addition, in Oakland, Berkeley, and Alameda. Clubs—all but two of which had been burned—leased large houses uptown. Many landlords took advantage of the situation to charge exorbitant rents, but the demand for space was so great that the tenants paid without protest. About the middle of May a publishing firm issued a "Relief Business Directory" containing the provisional addresses of four thousand commercial and professional offices, and announced that supplements would be printed at frequent intervals.

The disaster happened to occur during the Easter vacation of the public schools. As at least half of the school buildings had been either totally destroyed by fire or seriously damaged by the earthquake, and as thousands of children had left the city with their families, the Board of Education announced that the school year was at an end and the new term would not be-

1906

gin until August 1. When the schools did reopen, the shortage of buildings obliged the pupils to double up for the next two or three years, one school occupying the premises in the mornings, another in the afternoons.

To prevent financial chaos and avoid disastrous runs on the banks, Governor Pardee declared the three days following the earthquake to be legal holidays, and then extended the holidays for a month. This moratorium enabled the banks and commercial firms to allow their superheated vaults to cool off until they could be safely opened, postponed the fulfillment of contracts, and gave debtors time to meet their obligations. Early in June a special session of the legislature passed bills prolonging the duration of contracts to July 10 and extending the statute of limitations to the end of the year. During the moratorium many people in San Francisco had no cash except what they happened to have in their pockets on the morning of April 18, but they needed very little. There was not much to buy in the first few weeks, and the refugees could obtain free shelter, clothing, bedding, and (if they were really destitute) food. In order to enable employers to pay out small sums to their employees so that the latter might become independent of relief as soon as possible, San Francisco banks were permitted to deposit sums of any denomination with the United States Subtreasury in New York, which placed equal amounts to their credit at the San Francisco Mint. With these funds a "San Francisco Clearing House Bank" was opened on May 1 at the Mint, through which merchants and other responsible depositors in local banks could cash checks up to five hundred dollars. Each bank furnished one teller to handle its withdrawals; but in a few days the demand for cash dwindled to such an extent that on May 10 the *Chronicle* announced that "one teller at the Clearing-house bank in the Mint is able to pay all these orders . . . transact all new or special business, and have leisure beside. As illustrating the surplus of coin on hand . . . one of the country banks had

1906

$250,000 in currency brought from the East in a carpet sack. . . . On Tuesday the bank wired the money back to New York, as it had no use for it here."

Substantial sums did in fact flow into San Francisco during the moratorium. Families and friends in other cities sent gifts or loans of cash, and many local business firms received unexpected and unsolicited remittances from sympathetic out-of-town debtors. The Clearing House Bank was abolished on May 22, and on the following day most of the commercial and savings banks reopened, many of them in the relatively undamaged basements of their old quarters, where the vaults encased in solid masonry were intact. Other banks speedily erected one-story wooden shacks surrounding their exposed vaults and announced that they were ready for business. "It was banking in the rough," commented the *Chronicle,* "but real, regular banking."[18] The local banks, anticipating a flood of withdrawals after the long moratorium, had imported more than forty-six million dollars in gold from New York and Europe; but they soon returned the money. So firm was the confidence of San Franciscans in the stability of their financial institutions that, from the first day of the banks' reopening, deposits exceeded withdrawals, and by July the bank clearings actually showed an increase over those for the same month in the previous year.

In the intense heat of the conflagration, which reached 2200 degrees Fahrenheit in some places, more than eighty percent of the supposedly fireproof safes belonging to commercial firms failed to provide any protection whatever; their contents were reduced to ashes. Vaults encased in hollow tile fared little better. Fortunately the banks and some of the larger mercantile houses were equipped with strong steel vaults surrounded by solidly constructed brick walls. Practically all of these remained intact. The experience of Baltimore, where tons of valuable papers and records burst into flame with the rush of air into the hot interiors of vaults

The vault of the First National Bank at Bush and Sansome withstood the fire.

opened prematurely after the fire of February 1904, had warned San Francisco bankers and merchants to allow their surviving vaults to cool completely. Nearly all remained closed for three or four weeks, and when they were finally opened, with many precautions and in the presence of firemen armed with extinguishers, the contents were found, with only one or two exceptions, to be undamaged.

1906

Throughout the emergency period the inhabitants of San Francisco remained, on the whole, remarkably cheerful. "The people," reported the *Chronicle* six days after the earthquake, "are taking things as happily and philosophically as if they were out on a summer's camping trip." Few complained of the discomforts of life in a city without electricity, gas, transportation, running water, or shops, a city of bread lines and homeless refugees. They took the inconveniences in their stride and even managed to turn them into jokes. A rash of humorous signs testified to the irrepressible high spirits of the community. One sidewalk kitchen about the size of a dog kennel bore the crudely lettered notice: "Un-Fairmont Hotel. Open all night. Will exchange for country property." Another exhorted: "Eat, drink, and be merry, for tomorrow we may have to go to Oakland." One firm placed a sign in front of its completely demolished salesrooms explaining that it had moved because the elevator was not running; another that it had vacated the premises "because of alterations in the building on the eighteenth of April."[19] The musical instruments salvaged by many refugees, which at first appeared to be uesless burdens, proved excellent boosters of morale. Guitars, mandolins, accordions kept the campers entertained during the long hours of idleness. On the first night of the fire an unknown pianist, surrounded by a group of enthusiastic singers, gave an impromptu concert in Union Square and continued to play until the flames drove performers and audience to a safer neighborhood—though at least one cynical bystander ascribed this exhibition of hilarity to overindulgence in red wine. Three days after the earthquake a refugee was discovered near the entrance to Golden Gate Park, sitting on a cracker box and

~~

playing ragtime on an upright piano which he must have pushed through the streets for miles. His most popular selection was "Home Ain't Nothing Like This."

In general the citizens maintained excellent order. They accepted without question the restrictions imposed by the military, the National Guard, the regular police force, and the hastily organized citizens' patrols. Those who had houses to stay in obeyed the curfew rule (which lasted only a few days) as well as the orders concerning lights. Until the electric and gas services were restored, only candles were permitted in dwellings, as oil lamps were too dangerous. At first all lights had to be extinguished at ten o'clock; ten days after the earthquake the mayor postponed the onset of compulsory darkness until eleven, and on May 2 announced that candles could be allowed to burn all night.

The immediate closing of all saloons had an excellent effect on public order as well as on public health; but apparently it was not a blessing to everyone. "Many habitual drinkers, suddenly deprived of their accustomed stimulant, have been driven temporarily insane," the *Chronicle* announced on May 9. Members of exclusive clubs were able for about three weeks to order drinks at the bars of their temporary clubhouses. But to prevent the surreptitious reopening of the saloons, the authorities revoked all liquor licenses on May 12; and as the clubs required licenses, they were forced to close their bars. "It was awful dry,"[20] lamented the *Chronicle* reporter, presumably a club member himself.

General Greely reported, "The conduct of the community was conspicuous by its tranquility." More surprising was the continued good order for the ensuing two and a half months, and the lack of disorder and violence when the saloons finally reopened.

The commandeering of vehicles by the Committee of Fifty for the distribution of food and other supplies aroused a good deal of resentment and was discontinued after the first week. One energetic volunteer had been almost too successful in forcing private conveyances into public service. "Attorney Will Denman," the *Chronicle* reported on April 25, "to whom was assigned the task of securing teams, and who captured twenty-three fine carriage teams on Sacramento street the first night out, finished his work yesterday by trying to impress the Morgue wagon, his 123d team in three days. When he discovered that the last was a dead wagon he allowed it to pass." Thereafter, hired drays and wagons made deliveries to the relief stations.

"Perhaps never in the history of the city," the same paper declared on May 4, "has there been so little crime. . . . It is the opinion of the police that most of the criminal element has left the city." This was probably true, but there was certainly some looting and robbery, chiefly in the ruined area and at the docks and terminals. A detachment of marines from the cruiser *Chicago* was reported to have arrested twenty young men engaged in stealing copper and other metals at Meiggs Wharf. Extensive looting of relief supplies from freight cars in the Southern Pacific yards continued for several days, until mounted troops were assigned to guard the shipments. Among the false rumors current in the days immediately following the earthquake were grisly accounts by the inevitable "eyewitnesses" of hundreds of criminals shot by patrols and left unburied in the gutters. The actual number of deaths by shooting was nine, according to General Greely, who added with justifiable pride that the regular army had not been responsible for any of them. Five of the slain, unidentified in official or newspaper reports, were presumably authentic looters or thieves caught red-handed by patrols and summarily executed in conformity with the Mayor's peremptory but illegal proclamation. All of these killings occurred during the confusion of the first three or four days. Thereafter the authorities devised less drastic methods for the discouragement of looting: "Under guard of a squad of police-

1906

men, armed with shotguns, the older male offenders were put to work in clearing the streets of debris for from three to five hours, or until they dropped from fatigue, while the children were lectured severely and the women warned that if they appeared at headquarters again they would be compelled to wash dishes and the soiled linen of the police."[21]

Naturally so spectacular a catastrophe drew thousands of sightseers to the burned district, from nearby towns as well as from the city itself, as soon as the ashes cooled. Many of these visitors casually picked up souvenirs—sometimes quite valuable ones—from the ruins. On May 21 the police decided to discriminate between real looters and the merely thoughtless relic hunters. The latter escaped with a scolding for the first offense; the former were given regular trials and, if guilty, condemned to shovel debris for a specified number of days.

The other four victims of violence were not looters; according to reports in the local newspapers they were killed without justification by undisciplined, trigger-happy members of the militia or citizens' patrols. In spite of the closing of the saloons, liquor allegedly played a part in two or possibly three of these unfortunate fatalities.

On the night of April 19, Corporal Jacob H. Steinman of the National Guard of California shot Joseph Myers, superintendent of the children's playground in Columbia Square. Steinman, said by several witnesses to have been drunk, quarreled with Myers and ordered him to leave the park; when the superintendent protested and displayed his special policeman's badge, the militiaman fired twice, killing Myers almost instantly.

The murder of Frank Riordan (or Reardon) on the following afternoon seems to have been provoked, at least to some extent, by the victim himself. Near the corner of Post and Octavia streets, Riordan, a veteran of the Philippine campaign in the Spanish-American War, engaged in an alter-

1906

cation with a militiaman named Merriweather. Riordan, who according to some witnesses, had been drinking (though this was denied by others), sneered at the militia as "tin soldiers who had never smelled powder." A fistfight ensued, during which another National Guardsman, Lawrence N. Bechtel, who knew nothing about the cause of the quarrel, ran to his colleague's assistance and threatened Riordan with his bayonet. When Riordan seized the gun, Bechtel shot him.

The third incident was more complicated and involved some very peculiar circumstances. At about five in the afternoon on April 20, at Battery and Lombard streets close to the waterfront, an elderly man, probably a laborer, picked up a couple of live chickens and started to carry them away. He was not looting; the chickens had been liberated from a freight car, in which they would soon have died of hunger or thirst, by their owner, who invited the bystanders to help themselves. Ernest H. Denicke, a young civil and mining engineer and retired captain in the National Guard who had been assigned to duty on the waterfront, ordered a marine sentry to round up a gang to fight the fire. The sentry, who (in the opinion of numerous spectators) was very drunk, commanded the laborer to drop the fowls and take his place at the hose. The old man, apparently confused, hesitated for a moment, then released the chickens and walked away. Denicke instructed the marine to prod the workman with his bayonet; the man seized the gun, which the marine was too intoxicated to hold. Denicke, seeing that the sentry had been disarmed, fired three or four shots from his revolver. The old man fell and, for some two hours, lay in a pool of blood on the pavement before he died. A watchman placed a mattress under him, but nothing else was done to relieve his suffering. The corpse remained in the street until the following morning, when it was weighted with scrap iron and thrown into the bay. One witness reported the incident to the Committee of Fifty, but for some reason no attempt was made to investigate

1906

the killing or even to identify the officer until five weeks later, when the police started an inquiry and the newspapers printed the first accounts. Denicke then gave himself up; he admitted that he had shot the unknown man but denied that the marine had been drunk and claimed that the laborer had seized the weapon without provocation. The engineer was charged with murder and released on bail to await trial. A few weeks later the police fished up the body of the slain workman, whose name was never learned.

The fourth case of needless killing, and the one that aroused the greatest indignation because of the popularity and social prominence of the victim, was the shooting of Heber Cady Tilden, a commission merchant. As a member of the Committee of Fifty Tilden had devoted the first three days after the earthquake to relief work. On Sunday, April 22, he drove his three children and their nurse in his car to his country house at Menlo Park, approximately thirty miles south of San Francisco. He returned to the city about midnight accompanied by Hugo Altschul, a coachman, and Russel G. Seaman, an acting lieutenant in the army signal corps. As the car crossed 28th and Guerrero streets it was challenged by a citizens' patrol, but when one of the occupants shouted: "Red Cross!" the party was permitted to pass. The car did in fact carry two Red Cross flags, and Tilden wore an armband of the same organization; but these symbols might not have been visible in the unlighted streets. Three blocks farther on another patrol challenged the car and again allowed it to proceed without stopping. At Guerrero and 22nd a third patrol attempted to halt the car, and when the driver failed to obey, three members of the "vigilance committee" opened fire. One bullet struck Tilden in the back; he slumped in his seat and died in a few minutes. Meanwhile Seaman, who was armed, had swung out on the running board and fired five shots at the patrol without hitting anyone. The police immediately arrested the civilian guards who

1906

~~

had shot at the car: Edward S. Boynton, a telephone inspector; George W. Simmons, a marine engineer; and Malcolm T. Vance, a clerk. During the preliminary hearing it developed that the patrol had been organized by H. B. Walmsley, who in turn had received written authorization from Col. Walter N. Kelly of the First Regiment of the National Guard. Both testified that they had instructed the patrol to watch for fires, stop all suspicious characters, and prevent looting, but that they had issued orders to shoot only in self-defense. The three defendants were charged with murder and held for trial.

The unwarranted killings of Myers, Riordan, and Tilden were instantly followed by insistent demands for the abolition of all civilian patrols and the withdrawal of the National Guard. The chief of police promptly dissolved the "vigilance committees" on April 29, but Governor Pardee ignored Mayor Schmitz's protests and kept the militia on duty until the end of May. None of the defendants in the four cases was convicted. In September a Superior Court jury, after listening to much conflicting evidence, acquitted Steinman. Later that month another jury acquitted Vance and Simmons, and the court dismissed the charges against Boynton. At the end of November Denicke was acquitted, and a week later the assistant district attorney, realizing that no San Francisco jury would convict any patrol members who had committed murder or manslaughter during the confusion of the emergency period, requested and obtained the dismissal of the charge against Bechtel.

1906

Three days after the earthquake the United Cigar Stores Company ran a conspicuous advertisement in the San Francisco newspapers: "We have had ten of our stores and a warehouse destroyed in San Francisco. . . . We have sent ten of our best men . . . with orders to open TWENTY new stores immediately. . . . We believe it will be a better and greater city than ever, and we will back our judgment with our money." Similar expressions of confidence in the speedy reconstruction of the ruined city came from hundreds of prominent businesses, not only in California but all over the country. These were not merely pious wishes; announcements of applications for building permits, of intentions to rebuild as rapidly as possible and on a larger scale than before, appeared in all the papers during the first few weeks. Not for a moment did anyone suggest that the city might not recover from the calamity. As soon as people had a chance to catch their breaths, to evaluate the widespread destruction, and to face cheerfully but without illusions the immense labor before them, an extraordinary optimism spread throughout the entire community.

The first task was to clear the streets in the burned area. Almost every thoroughfare was choked with rubble, which made the distribution of urgently needed provisions and supplies extremely difficult. Moreover the intense heat had ruined the pavements, and tottering walls lining the streets endangered the lives of pedestrians and workers. During the first days any able-bodied male walking along Mission Street—the first important downtown street to be cleared— was apt to find himself peremptorily ordered by patrols to pick up a shovel and help in the removal of debris. The majority accepted the chore good-humoredly and took care to

Clearing the site of the Palace Hotel.

avoid the neighborhood in future. But the patrols, especially those organized by the militia, manifested more zeal than discrimination, so that the mayor was obliged to protest to the commanding officer: "A great number of complaints have come in . . . relative to arrests by your National Guard of reputable citizens in the employ of the city and even doctors and officials . . . and pressing them into service for work upon the public streets. Such action is absolutely illegal. . . ."[22] Thereafter the work was performed by paid laborers, later supplemented by a small force of convicted looters. Gangs of workmen, aided by the few available steam-shovels, cleared most of Mission and Market streets within a few days, while army artillerymen, assisted by civilians, dynamited the unsafe remnants of flanking walls. "There will not be a dangerous ruin standing in Market Street by this afternoon," the *Examiner* announced six days after the earthquake. Ten days later most of the streets in the wholesale, retail, and financial districts north of Market Street were open to traffic, though the pavements were badly cracked and full of holes. An even greater undertaking, though not quite so urgent, was the removal of mountains of debris, estimated at over ten million cubic yards, from the building sites covering about five hundred city blocks. To expedite this work the railroads laid temporary tracks along several of the more important streets and hauled the rubble in open freight cars to a dump in a cove of San Francisco Bay. When this was completely filled, the carloads were discharged into two-thousand-ton barges which were towed to the vicinity of Mile Rock and dumped into the ocean. A good deal of the twisted iron and steel was salvaged and sold for scrap.

With almost incredible speed the various public utility companies began to overhaul their wrecked installations and restore service. Within three days the San Andreas conduit, the least severely damaged of the four supplying water to the city, had been patched sufficiently to permit water to flow into a few sections, and less than a month later the supply in the unburned districts was almost normal. Inspection and repair of the sewers took only a week. Fortunately one of the electric company's principal power plants, situated far from the destroyed area, had survived. Electric lights were burning along the waterfront six days after the earthquake, and in another week electric street lighting functioned throughout the unburned residence sections. The flow of electricity into private dwellings proceeded more slowly, as all connections had to be inspected and, if necessary, repaired; but by May 1 some houses in the Western Addition had electric light, and within two more weeks—less than a month after the earthquake—the restoration of service was practically completed.

Testing of gas mains and fixtures took still more time, though the inspectors found only about one half of one percent of the installations to be seriously damaged. One cause of delay, as reported in the *Chronicle,* was the "contemptible swindle worked here and there by rogues pretending to be in the employ of the company and charging all they could collect

1906

~~~

for inspecting and turning on. The police have . . . arrested a few of these frauds and the company has succeeded in scaring several such gangs out of their disreputable business." More than three weeks elapsed before the first households received gas for cooking and lighting; ten days later practically all fixtures were in working order.

A few hours after the earthquake the army signal corps installed and operated an emergency telegraph system connecting military headquarters, hospitals, and relief stations within the city. Telephone communication with Oakland was re-established in a week, but at first only for official and business calls. By May 1 the telephone company had restored service to about one thousand instruments in the unburned district, and soon connected up the remainder.

The United Railroads resumed operation of electric streetcars on Fillmore Street in the Western Addition three days after the earthquake, but withdrew them the next day at the mayor's request, ostensibly because of possible danger of fire from damaged wires. After five days of idleness the Fillmore Street cars again started to run. Meanwhile the company had been working night and day to rebuild one of its lines through the burned district to the Ferry Building. Before the earthquake most of the streetcars in San Francisco had been hauled by underground cables on account of the very steep hills; but by 1906 improvements in electric traction made possible the replacement of the picturesque but slow little cable cars by more capacious and economical trolleys on many of the less precipitous routes. For some years the United Railroads had contemplated a number of such conversions, especially on relatively level Market Street, from which half a dozen cable lines branched off at various intersections to serve different parts of the city. The municipal authorities had long been in favor of the proposed alteration, but had insisted upon the installation of underground power lines on Market Street instead of the cheaper but unsightly overhead

1906

〜〜

wires. The United Railroads, which naturally preferred the
less costly alternative, promptly took advantage of the disrup-
tion caused by the earthquake and fire to carry out its own
project. All of the old cable machinery was out of commission, and its rehabilitation would have been much slower and
more expensive than an immediate change to an electric system. Four days after the earthquake Mayor Schmitz sur-
prised the citizens of San Francisco by announcing that he
had granted to the United Railroads the very concession he
had previously refused to consider: a franchise for an overhead trolley line on Market Street. Back of this sudden
change of heart lay a sordid story of bribery and corruption
which subsequently resulted in the indictment of the mayor,
several supervisors, United Railroad officials, and the politi-
cal boss Abraham Ruef. But that unsavory scandal, followed
by a violent municipal upheaval and the election of a reform
administration, did not come into the open until about a year
later; though even at the time of the award many people sus-
pected, and one or two newspapers hinted at, some kind of
skulduggery.

It must be admitted that the franchise, however ini-
quitous the method by which it was obtained, did greatly
expedite the restoration of public transportation and the reconstruction of the city. The United Railroads speedily
erected poles and strung overhead wires, and five days after
the granting of the new franchise it began to operate electric
cars, partly on Mission Street and partly on Market, to the
ferries. At the same time the company resumed trolley service
on several existing routes in the unburned districts, and as
soon as the streets were cleared and dangerous walls blown
up it extended its lines in the downtown areas. Within three
weeks after the earthquake, the United Railroads had 250
electric cars in service and had reopened all of its trolley lines
in the sections untouched by the fire. It took much longer to
repair those cable systems which had to be retained because

1906

electric cars could not negotiate the excessively steep grades on certain streets. During the first few days the United Railroads carried refugees on its trolleys free of charge, and also transported their salvaged property, if any. Thereafter for a brief period the company charged regular five-cent fares but donated the receipts to the relief fund.

The one exception to the speed and efficiency of the restoration of something approaching normal living conditions was in the field of chimney inspection. About eighty thousand chimneys required inspection and, in many instances, repairs before householders could obtain permits to dismantle their sidewalk kitchens and resume indoor cooking. For this purpose the unburned sections of the city were divided into fifteen districts, each served by ten to fifteen inspectors. The test for damage, according to the *Chronicle,* "is the severest known and is called the smoke test. It is operated by putting a wet sack over the top of the flue and building a smudge at the bottom of sulphur and other malodorous inflammables. If there is a crack . . . it will soon be discovered by the coughing of the inspector and his aids." But the cough test did not get under way in private dwellings until five weeks after the earthquake, and then it dragged on for two months or longer. Householders complained bitterly about the delay, and many alleged (probably with a good deal of truth) that chimney inspections, instead of being made in the order in which applications were filed, were speeded up for those who handed out liberal bribes and slowed down for residents unwilling to submit to extortion.

The military and the Relief Corporation soon brought about significant improvements in the hastily organized refugee camps. As quickly as possible they abolished most of the one hundred or more small scattered camps, difficult to supervise and to maintain in sanitary condition, and attempted to concentrate the occupants in a few large official communities, some under military control and some under that of the Relief Corporation. But many of the refugees refused to move to the official camps, and as the police proved unwilling to dislodge them forcibly the regrouping did not take place as rapidly or as completely as the authorities desired. On August 1, when the army turned over the supervision of its camps to the corporation, the official camps harbored about eighteen thousand persons and the unofficial ones ten to fifteen thousand. In the official camps, most of which were situated in the Presidio and Golden Gate Park, no restrictions were imposed except a few fundamental rules governing order, decency, and cleanliness; habitual offenders against any of these regulations were ejected and refused admission to any other official camp. The larger camps provided excellent toilet facilities, laundries, and bathhouses with hot and cold running water. The corporation constructed wooden buildings for the accommodation of kindergartens, day nurseries, reading rooms, sewing classes, clubs, religious meetings, lectures, concerts, and other social purposes. A few temporary schools were established to guard the children from what General Greely called "the lowering tendencies of camp life" and incidentally to keep them out of mischief for a few hours a day.

During July and August (cold windy months in San Francisco) the tents in the official camps were floored with wood. But tents were too flimsy for comfortable habitation in the rainy winter. Between September 1906 and March 1907 the Relief Corporation erected about fifty-six hundred prefabricated wooden cottages, of which more than four thousand contained three rooms and the rest two rooms each, at a cost of approximately $55 per room. In addition the corporation built in South Park a group of nineteen two-story tenements with a bathhouse and laundry. The original proposal to charge a monthly rental of six dollars for a three-room and four dollars for a two-room cabin proved impracticable because the mayor opposed the collection of rent for dwellings

1906

~~

located in city parks, and the Board of Supervisors passed a special ordinance declaring such rents illegal. The corporation then substituted a contract of sale whereby the occupant agreed to buy his cottage and pay for it in monthly installments equal in amount to the proposed rental. These sums were subsequently refunded to those who purchased lots on which to place their cottages after the camps broke up. Taking advantage of these generous terms, the refugees bought more than ninety-five percent of the cabins and moved them to purchased or rented lots in various sections of the city. The cost of moving, borne by the owner or in some instances by the Associated Charities, varied from twelve dollars to twenty-five dollars. Some tenants with large families bought two or three cottages and combined them into fairly commodious permanent residences. By August 1907 all of the camps had been closed except one in Lobos Square near Fort Mason, which was retained until June 1908 for the benefit of about one thousand of the poorest refugees.

For approximately three years after the earthquake and fire the word most frequently heard in San Francisco was "temporary." Almost everything was temporary: the locations of buildings, the buildings themselves, installations and makeshifts of all kinds. The telephone company even named a new exchange in the burned district "Temporary."

During the period of reconstruction the entire retail shopping district, as well as many other commercial enterprises, moved uptown. Fillmore Street, previously a rather shabby thoroughfare of small neighborhood shops, suddenly blossomed into an important business center. Before the fire had burned itself out, merchants were signing leases for stores in the new section, and during the next week they began to remodel and enlarge the existing premises and to erect new buildings. "It is not easy to move along Fillmore Street at present," the *Chronicle* reported two weeks after the earth-

The temporary Emporium on Van Ness Avenue.

quake, "as the sidewalks are thronged with people and the roadway [is] filled with all sorts of vehicles. A box or a plank is enough for many a cigar and tobacco dealer to do business on; an optician who was burned out has his present stock displayed on a fence. . . . A great variety of signs are up. . . . The spelling is generally according to Webster, but in some places there are indications that the painter's dictionary was lost in the flames."[23] Very little salable merchandise of any kind remained in the city, but the temporary stores were quickly stocked with goods which had been in transit from eastern cities at the time of the earthquake and which were delivered after a brief delay, and a little later with commodities ordered by telegraph.

Another shopping center quickly sprang up along Valencia Street and other thoroughfares in the unburned sections of the Mission district; but the principal department stores and smart specialty shops established temporary quarters on Van Ness Avenue at the western edge of the destroyed area. The Retail Merchants' Association leased whole blocks on both sides of the avenue (a few still occupied

1906

~~

by undamaged houses but for the most part filled with
nothing but rubble and ashes) and allotted them to its members according to their needs. Less than three weeks after the
earthquake, the Emporium, the largest department store in
the city, opened for business in an old residence on Van Ness
Avenue and began rapidly covering the scorched lawns and
gardens with wooden salesrooms. The City of Paris, the
White House, and numerous other big firms erected stores in
the neighborhood. Within three months a solid mile of retail
shops, housed in unpretentious wooden buildings but display-
ing the same costly luxuries that they had offered before the
fire, lined both sides of Van Ness Avenue from McAllister to
Washington Street.

1906

San Francisco has always been, and still is, a pleasure-loving city. Its inhabitants cheerfully put up with all the temporary discomforts and inconveniences forced on them by the disaster, but not even a violent earthquake and a devastating conflagration could make them renounce their customary entertainments and social activities for a moment longer than was absolutely necessary. On the third Sunday the First Regiment of the National Guard gave a band concert in Golden Gate Park, though the great stone bandstand had been partially wrecked by the earthquake and the tents of refugees covered the surrounding lawns. Two weeks later the Orpheum, the leading vaudeville theater, resumed regular twice-a-day performances in temporary quarters at the Chutes, which reopened all of the attractions in its amusement park on the same day. The managements of the Central Theater (formerly consecrated to lurid melodrama) and of the more sedate Majestic Theater combined to purchase the huge tent, complete with stage and bleachers seating six thousand, used by Sarah Bernhardt on her recent tour; they also bought a second large tent and announced that both would be erected on Market Street, one for vaudeville, the other for "farce comedies." Among the first building permits applied for was one for the construction of a new fireproof theater one block from Fillmore Street. Other new theaters quickly sprang up in the same neighborhood, which also furnished temporary sites for many of the restaurants and cafes for which San Francisco had long been noted.

During the summer the Hotel St. Francis opened a temporary annex across the street in Union Square, a one-story wooden structure containing two hundred guest rooms,

Union Square, from the corner of Post and Powell streets.

and installed a grillroom in the quickly repaired basement of the main hotel while the work of reconstruction continued on the gutted but structurally sound floors above. The Palace Hotel erected a simple wooden building at Post and Leavenworth streets, on the southern slope of Nob Hill, which boasted a "ballroom;" and this makeshift apartment, together with the Paris Tea Garden adjoining the temporary Van Ness Avenue store of the City of Paris, served as the centers of fashionable social life until the luxurious Fairmont Hotel, only superficially damaged when the fire swept through its unfinished interior, opened on April 18, 1907, the first anniversary of the earthquake. The roofless walls of the old Palace on Market Street remained standing in excellent condition and could have been restored to use; but the building, though little more than thirty years old, was already out-of-date; the rooms were too large and the ceilings too high for economical operation. The owners therefore tore down the solid walls and constructed an entirely new hotel on the same site with a more or less similar floor plan featuring a great central court, a modified version of the famous original. Within a few weeks

1906

~~

after the earthquake, social notes and gossip in the newspapers began to replace the lists of changed addresses and the
appeals for information concerning missing relatives and
friends, though for some time the social items consisted of little more than news of traveling San Franciscans and announcements of engagements and weddings.

For more than a year the complicated problems of insurance
preoccupied San Francisco property owners. The fire had destroyed many policies stowed in defective safes and vaults, so
that some of the insured found it difficult to prove their losses.
It was also discovered that some policies contained "earthquake clauses" in fine print which few people had taken the
trouble to read carefully. These clauses relieved the companies of liability for damage caused, in some cases directly, in
others indirectly, by earthquake; and a few companies, claim-
ing exemption because the earthquake had caused the conflagration, refused to pay any part of the amount due. Others,
ascribing part of the damage to the earthquake and part to
the fire, arbitrarily divided the city into zones and agreed to
pay twenty-five cents on the dollar in some areas, fifty or
seventy-five cents in others. Such fractional settlements might
not have been unreasonable had it been possible to establish
with any degree of accuracy the relative amount of destruction caused by each of the two calamities; but in most instances there was actually no way in which either the owner
or the insurance company could estimate, much less prove,
how much damage the earthquake had done to any specific
building before the flames destroyed it a few hours later. The
chief offenders were four or five German and one or two
English and American firms. But the great majority of insurance companies, American and foreign, paid up promptly
and in full. The combined liabilities aggregated about
$170,600,000; the amount actually paid was about
$163,700,000. Of course this sum did not go far to compen-

1906

sate for a total property loss of approximately $500,000,000; nevertheless it saved a great many businesses from bankruptcy and made possible the rapid rehabilitation of the city. The destruction of records caused property owners to fear that their titles to real estate might be challenged; but the passage of the McEnerney Act by a special session of the legislature averted this danger. The act provided that any owner, confronted by a rival claimant and unable to show a deed, could establish title by the production in court of other satisfactory evidence. There were in fact few attempts to gain possession of property by fraud.

Meanwhile the rebuilding of the city proceeded at a feverish pace. Architects built or rented temporary quarters, hired extra draftsmen, and turned out plans and specifications as fast as possible. Contractors had more work than they could handle. Within a month, twenty-five thousand men were employed in the building trades. The demand for the services of carpenters, steelworkers, plumbers, glaziers, electricians, painters, and cabinetmakers grew day by day. Wages and the cost of materials soared, but the high prices failed to retard the work of reconstruction. San Francisco had been a rich city, and in spite of the staggering property loss it was still prosperous. Insurance payments poured in; landlords raised their rents; shopkeepers reaped a golden harvest. There was a rush to replace destroyed furniture, household gear, and clothing. Almost everyone seemed to have money to spend, not only on necessities but on luxuries. Three of the large steel and iron foundries, located in outlying districts, had survived and were furnishing employment to fifteen hundred men less than ten days after the earthquake.

The first buildings to be erected in the burned area were hundreds of temporary wooden structures, little more than shacks, which required no building permits. The next step was the rehabilitation of the gutted but otherwise undamaged office buildings. Within three months, eighteen of these had been partially or wholly reoccupied and thirty-five others were being rapidly put into serviceable condition. Less than six weeks after the earthquake the San Francisco Stock and Exchange Board, the Stock and Bond Exchange, and the Stock and Oil Exchange reopened in the basement and lower floors of the burned-out Merchants' Exchange Building on California Street. In August the *Chronicle* terminated its lease in Oakland and resumed publication in its own building at Kearny and Market streets, to be followed shortly afterwards by the *Call* in the restored basement of the Spreckels Building and the *Examiner* in temporary quarters pending construction of the new Hearst Building on its original site. At the same time new permanent structures were being planned and erected in every part of the burned district. Nearly two thousand building permits were issued in the first two months. Within three years the 28,000 destroyed buildings had been replaced by 20,500 new ones, in general much more substantial than the old, at a cost of over $50,000,000 more than the total value of the ruined structures.

With few exceptions the financial institutions, wholesale firms, retail stores, theaters, and restaurants occupied new or rehabilitated buildings on or in the immediate vicinity of their former sites, but some sections of the city underwent drastic changes in character and appearance. Luxurious apartment houses, hotels, clubs, and non-residential buildings of various kinds superseded the old ornate mansions on Nob Hill. The destroyed Stanford house was replaced by a large eight-story apartment building, Stanford Court, which after some sixty years has in turn been converted into a first-class hotel. The jigsawed and turreted Mark Hopkins house next door, which had been given to the University of California years before the earthquake for use as an art institute, served the same purpose after the fire in the reduced space of the basement until it was supplanted about twenty years later by the present Mark Hopkins Hotel. The brownstone shell of

1906

~~

the James Flood residence was remodeled and enlarged for occupancy by the Pacific Union Club, and the adjoining Huntington property was transformed into a small public park. The Crocker heirs donated their square block to the Episcopal diocese as a site for the new Grace Cathedral. In another part of town the ruins of the jerry-built City Hall were razed, and several years later a handsome new City Hall and Civic Center were constructed a few blocks away. Across Van Ness Avenue from the City Hall a modern Opera House and Veterans' Building, containing an art museum, fill two blocks, and most recently a large concert hall has been added.

The reconstruction of Chinatown, completely destroyed by fire, gave rise to brief but heated controversy. At first some white San Franciscans proposed the removal of the Chinese to a new location in the neighborhood of Hunter's Point, a remote area in the extreme southeastern corner of the city, on the ground that the original site on the eastern slope of Nob Hill was much too valuable, as well as too close to the fashionable hotel and shopping districts, to be wasted on Asians. But the Chinese, many of whom owned property in their old quarter, vigorously opposed the project, and there was no legal method by which they could be forced to relinquish their real estate. Fortunately the agitation for their resettlement, which had never boasted more than a few prejudiced advocates, soon died down. The Chinese returned unmolested to ther former location. The new Chinatown, less mysterious and picturesque than the old unsavory warren but much tidier and more solidly constructed, is today one of the city's greatest tourist attractions.

A year or two before the earthquake the Chicago architect Daniel Hudson Burnham had drawn up a comprehensive plan for the improvement of San Francisco. The city had been laid out originally as a checkerboard of straight streets, without regard for the extreme height and steepness of the

1906

hills. The precipitous slopes constituted serious impediments to circulation; horse-drawn vehicles and the puny automobiles of the early years of this century often had to make long detours to reach the lofty summits, and a few of the steepest blocks are still closed by concrete barriers to even the powerful cars in use today. Burnham proposed, among many other praiseworthy reforms, the construction of several diagonal and curved avenues connecting the principal valleys and hilltops by relatively easy grades. His suggestions, or most of them, might have been adopted, to the great benefit of the city, had the earthquake and fire not intervened. Indeed the complete destruction of so large an area did seem to present the citizens with a most favorable opportunity to carry out the plan and cut new streets through the burned district without having to pay for the demolition of existing buildings. But the construction of new thoroughfares, even across empty blocks, would have entailed condemnation proceedings and protracted litigation. The property owners and businessmen were far too impatient to commence rebuilding to tolerate any avoidable delay. "Opposition to the 'cobwebby' plans for the beautification of San Francisco's down-town business streets is increasing daily," the *Chronicle* reported five weeks after the earthquake. So the shortsighted "practical" view prevailed; the city abandoned the Burnham project and lost its chance to revise its inconvenient and inappropriate street plan.

Towards the end of the first summer, when the food shops and temporary department stores had reopened and electric lights, gas appliances, telephones, indoor cooking stoves, running water, and streetcars were functioning more or less normally, most of the families whose houses remained intact returned to San Francisco from voluntary exile in the country and suburbs. They found a city vastly different from the desolate ruin they had left a few months before. The air was filled with the clatter of hammering and riveting, as well

116

as with clouds of ash and brick dust as steam and hand shovels cleared away the rubble and excavated for new foundations. San Francisco was filthy, but it was certainly lively. As building after building opened its doors in the burned district, the city gradually moved downtown again. Commercial firms gave up their temporary quarters in the Western Addition or Oakland and installed themselves in modern offices, factories, and warehouses. Hotels, theaters, restaurants, clubs, and retail stores reopened in new buildings smelling of fresh paint. In three years the reconstruction was practically complete, though there were still gaps in the rows of fine new structures. Fillmore Street managed to retain some of its importance as an uptown shopping center, but Van Ness Avenue was entirely deserted until, a little later, it was transformed into a street of ugly, strictly utilitarian salesrooms for motor cars and accessories.

During and after the rebuilding of the city a number of precautions were taken to prevent the recurrence of a similar disaster in the future. San Francisco is still, and always will be, subject to earthquakes, and a good many shocks have occurred from time to time, though none have approached in intensity the quake of 1906, and none have caused any appreciable damage. The lesson was well learned; nearly all of the new buildings, some of which are more than twice as high as the tallest that existed in 1906, are soundly constructed and sufficiently resilient to withstand violent shaking. The fire limits—the area within which only fireproof and fire-resistant structures are permitted—have been slightly extended, though wood is still generally used for private houses and for the crowded blocks of inexpensive flats that have sprung up in many districts. Among the measures taken to reduce the danger of another extensive conflagration are the construction of two large storage reservoirs and two distributing reservoirs within the city limits; the installation of valves and bypasses to detour water round defective mains; the purchase of fire-

boats; the building of pumping stations for both fresh and salt water; and the excavation of numerous salt-water cisterns at street intersections.

Almost no traces of the great earthquake and fire are visible today. One of the very few relics that have been deliberately preserved is a graceful Ionic portico, all that survived of the handsome Towne residence on Nob Hill. This monument, affectionately christened "Portals of the Past," has been transferred to Golden Gate Park, where its marble columns, silhouetted against a background of trees and shrubs, are reflected in the placid waters of a miniature lake.

The entrance portico of the Towne residence on California Street, between Taylor and Jones, the dome of City Hall can be seen in the distance (opposite). The same portico as it stands today in Golden Gate Park (above), where it is known as "Portals of the Past."

REFERENCE NOTES

1. David Starr Jordan, ed., *The California Earthquake of 1906* (San Francisco: A.M. Robertson, 1907), pp. 5, 15-19, 28-33.

2. William Knox Bronson, *The Earth Shook, the Sky Burned* (Garden City, N.Y.: Doubleday & Co., Inc., 1959), pp. 132-134.

3. Department of the Interior. United States Geological Survey, Bulletin No. 324, *The San Francisco Earthquake and Fire of April 18, 1906 and Their Effects on Structures and Structural Materials* (Washington, D.C.: U.S. Government Printing Office, 1907), p. 22.

4. *San Francisco Chronicle,* 3 May 1906, p. 14.

5. Frank W. Aitken and Edward Hilton, *A History of the Earthquake and Fire in San Francisco* (San Francisco: Edward Hilton Co., 1906), pp. 16, 204-205.

6. *Chronicle,* 24 April 1906, p. 1.

7. *Chronicle,* 27 April 1906, p. 2.

8. *New York Daily Tribune,* 24 April 1906, p. 3.

9. Sydney Tyler, *San Francisco's Great Disaster* (Philadelphia: P.W. Ziegler Co., 1906), p. 214.

10. James Russel Wilson, *San Francisco's Horror of Earthquake and Fire* (Philadelphia: National Publishing Co., 1906). Faked illustrations duplicated in Alexander P. Livingstone (compiler), *Complete Story of San Francisco's Terrible Calamity of Earthquake and Fire* (Continental Publishing House), n.p., n.d.

11. Adolphus Washington Greely, Major General, United States Army, *Earthquake in California, April 18, 1906. Special Report on the Relief Operations Conducted by the Military Authorities of the United States at San Francisco and Other Points* (Washington, D.C.: U.S. Government Printing Office, 1906), p. 46.

12. *San Francisco Examiner,* 21 April 1906, p. 1.

13. *Chronicle,* 11 May 1906, p. 8.

14. *The Argonaut,* 12 May 1906 (San Francisco), p. 1.

15. *Chronicle,* 3 May 1906, p. 2; 14 May 1906, p. 10.

16. Adolphus Washington Greely, *op cit.,* pp. 32–34.

17. Russell Sage Foundation, *San Francisco Relief Survey* (New York: Survey Associates, Inc., 1913), p. 55.

18. *Chronicle,* 24 May 1906, p. 1.

19. Frank W. Aitken and Edward Hilton, *op cit.,* pp. 181–182.

20. *Chronicle,* 13 May 1906, p. 17.

21. *Ibid.,* 12 May 1906, p. 1.

22. *Ibid.,* 25 April 1906, p. 2.

23. *Ibid.,* 3 May 1906, p. 15.

ABOUT THE AUTHOR

Gerstle Mack, the author of this vivid picture of San Francisco's calamitous earthquake and fire in April 1906, is a man of bewilderingly manifold talents, ranging from those of gifted architect and scenic designer to eloquent author, family historian and to the production of penetratingly critical biographies of such masters as Cézanne, Toulouse-Lautrec, and Courbet. He was born in San Francisco in 1894, the son of Adolph and Clara Gerstle Mack, both of them members of venerable San Francisco families. Following attendance at local public schools, Mack entered the University of California in Berkeley, studying architecture there from 1911 to 1915. He continued his studies in this field at the Massachusetts Institute of Technology during 1915-16. The following year he spent as a draftsman with the noted architectural firm of Warren & Wetmore in New York. In World War I he served as a 2nd and then 1st lieutenant in the U.S. Reserve Corps of Engineers in France in 1918-19, as Depot Engineer of Paris. Returning to San Francisco, he was a draftsman in the office of the eminent architect Willis Polk (1919-20) and became a junior partner in the Polk firm (1920-21). From 1922 to 1926 he was affiliated with the great theatrical designer Norman Bel Geddes in New York. For the better part of the years between 1926 and 1938, Mack lived in France and Spain. During the latter part of World War II (1944-45) he held a key post in London with the "Cloak and Dagger" outfit, technically the Office of Strategic Services. Mr. Mack has made his home in New York since 1938. But the years of his residence have been richly interlarded with worldwide travel. Meanwhile, he has been a frequent visitor to his native heath.

It is not surprising that Mack has been a faithful visitor to San Francisco, a city where for generations the Gerstles and the Macks have been deeply entrenched, civic-minded citizens. All four of his grandparents emigrated to the United States from southern Germany in the 1830s and 1840s. Lewis Gerstle, his maternal grandfather, came to California in 1850, settling in Sacramento where he went into partnership with Louis Sloss (another hallowed name in the annals of mid-nineteenth century San Francisco) as suppliers of staple goods, clothing, tools, etc. to the gold miners. He married Hannah Greenebaum in Philadelphia in 1858 and brought her to Sacramento, where their two oldest children were born, the second being Gerstle Mack's mother, born in June 1861.

The family moved to San Francisco early in 1862 after a disastrous flood in Sacramento. In 1868, the year after Alaska was purchased by the United States from Russia, Lewis Gerstle, Louis Sloss, and several other partners founded the Alaska Commercial Company, to which, in 1870, our government awarded the fur seal monopoly in the Pribiloff Islands in the Bering Sea for twenty years with a limit of one hundred thousand skins a year. Mack's father, born in New York in 1858, studied at the College of Pharmacy and came to California in 1875 at the age of seventeen. He first opened a small drugstore in Visalia and then moved to San Francisco, where he founded the wholesale drug firm of Mack & Company. Gerstle Mack's parents were married in San Francisco in 1882. He was by several years the youngest of four children. On the Gerstle side his family has lived in San Francisco for 119 years, and on the Mack side for more than a century.

At the time of the appalling events of April 1906, Gerstle Mack was not quite twelve years old; so as he has correctly observed, he must be one of the few people alive today who was old enough to remember those cataclysmic days seventy-five years ago. Thus his eyewitness observations assume unusual importance.

Some of the varied accomplishments of this gifted man stand out with great clarity. To those recounted above, the writer would like to add that of having a genius for *gourmet* cooking. It is of a caliber to make Escoffier stir uneasily in his grave.

THOMAS CARR HOWE, *Director Emeritus, California Palace of the Legion of Honor San Francisco.*

1906

~

INDEX

1906

1906

Presidio, 43, 46, 65, 69, 71, 75, 80–82, 106
prisoners, 81

Queen of Sheba (opera), 56

rain, 81–82
Rappold, Marie, 56
Red Cross, 83, 85–87, 98
Redwood City, 28
refugee camps, 69–72, 75–76, 81–82, 88, 105–107
Relief Corporation, 83–85, 105–106
Richter, Charles F., 35
Richter scale, 35
Riordan, Frank, 96–97, 99
Roanoke (steamer), 77
Roosevelt, President Theodore, 64, 78, 83
Ruef, Abraham, 104
Russell Sage Foundation, 79
Russian Hill, 47–48, 51

St. Dunstan Hotel, 58
St. Francis Hotel, 42, 54, 57, 110–111
saloons, 94, 96
San Andreas Fault, 23–30
San Andreas Lake, 27, 36–37, 102
San Andreas Valley, 27
San Diego, 60
San Jose, 28–29, 67, 73
San Juan Bautista, 24, 30
San Leandro, 72
San Mateo, 27
San Rafael, 11, 13–17, 72
Santa Cruz, 30
Santa Fe R.R., 73, 77
Santa Rosa, 26, 67
Sausalito, 13, 72
Schmitz, Mayor Eugene, 62–63, 67, 82, 99, 101, 103–104

schools, 11, 49, 89–90, 106
Scotti, Antonio, 56–57
Seal, A.B., 88
Seal, Sarah, 88
Seaman, Russel G., 98
Seattle, 75
Sembrich, Marcella, 56–58
Shreve Building, 54
Simmons, George W., 99
Sloss, Sarah, 12
Southern Pacific R.R., 51, 59, 72–74, 77
Spreckels (*Call*) Building, 33, 38, 54, 114
Spreckels (Claus) residence, 46
Stanford Court Hotel, 114
Stanford residence, 43, 114
Stanford University, 28
Steinman, Cpl. Jacob H., 96, 99
Stevens, Ashton, 56
Stock Exchanges, 114
street cars, 10, 12, 50, 68, 103–105, 116
Sullivan, Dennis T., 40–42

Taft, William Howard, 76
Telegraph Hill, 38, 47–48, 51–52
telegraph lines, 50, 59, 61, 66, 72, 76, 103, 108
telephones, 10, 13, 50, 59, 72, 103, 116
Tevis, Dr. Harry, 57, 59
theaters, 49, 110, 117
Tiburon, 13, 72
Tilden, Heber Cady, 98–99
Tokyo, 55
Tomales Bay, 25–26
Towne residence, 118
tsunamis (tidal waves), 26, 60
Tully, Madame, 88

Union Square, 42, 93, 110

1906

~